Hollywood BACHELOR PADS

Carol Kipling

Schiffer Publishing Ltd

4880 Lower Valley Road Atglen, Pennsylvania 19310

Printed in China

Library of Congress Control Number: 2009925838

Covers and book designed by: Bruce Waters
Cover photo by Julius Schulman and Juergen Nogai of architecture by SPF Architects
Type set in Huminist

ISBN: 978-0-7643-3307-1
Printed in China

Published by Schiffer Publishing Ltd.
4880 Lower Valley Road
Atglen, PA 19310
Phone: (610) 593-1777; Fax: (610) 593-2002
E-mail: Info@schifferbooks.com

In Europe, Schiffer books are distributed by
Bushwood Books
6 Marksbury Ave.
Kew Gardens
Surrey TW9 4JF England
Phone: 44 (0) 20 8392 8585; Fax: 44 (0) 20 8392 9876
E-mail: info@bushwoodbooks.co.uk
Website: www.bushwoodbooks.co.uk

Contents

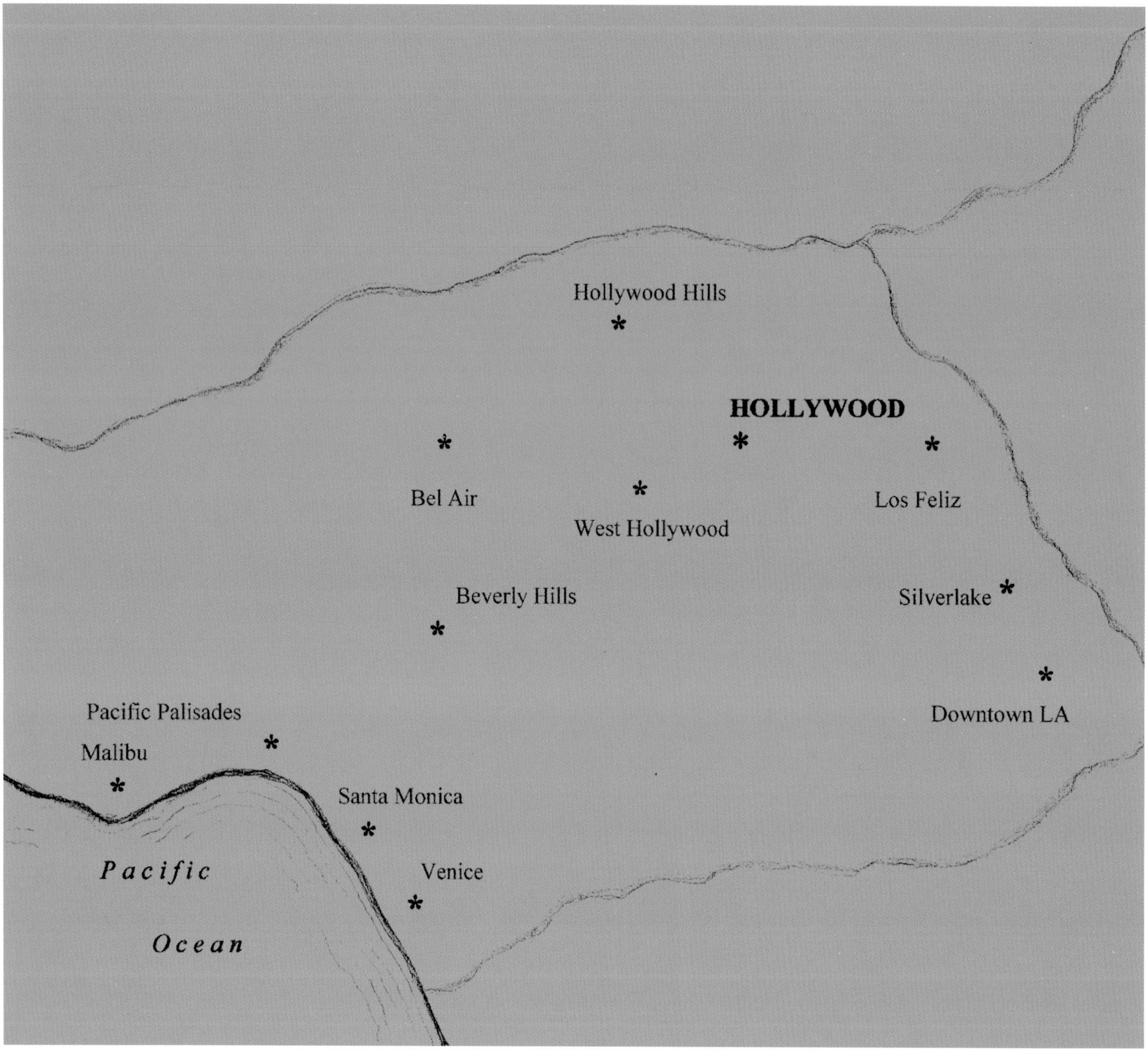
Hollywood Hills
HOLLYWOOD
Bel Air
West Hollywood
Los Feliz
Beverly Hills
Silverlake
Downtown LA
Pacific Palisades
Malibu
Santa Monica
Venice
Pacific
Ocean

Acknowledgements

Creating film, television, and all other forms of entertainment requires the orchestrated efforts of many talented people. Likewise, this book needed many skilled hands, hearts, and minds to help it come to fruition. My humble thanks to those who made this possible: Stanley Anderson, Lori Bush, Trace Beaulieu, Cindy Canzoneri, Collin Ferrell, Charlie Fine, Kevin Gill, Art Gray, Simon Halls, Tom Heinz, Alex Hendler, Nancy Janusz Lindsey, Patricia Judice, Karrison Krasowski, Shaunery Krasowski, Randell Makinson, John Marcom, Kristafer Michael, Jonathan Otis, Tom Petty, Linda Rahn, Janet Sager, Tina Skinner, Jon Thorsen, Anna Tseklenis, David Tseklenis, Harold Tseklenis, Jamie Weiss, Michael T. Weiss, and Morgan Wandell.

Introduction

The original HOLLYWOODLAND sign, circa 1923.

When Howard Hughes – once the richest bachelor in the United States – decided to produce movies, he settled into a magnificent mansion near Hollywood. It overlooked the Wilshire Country Club, in the same neighborhood where I moved more than 50 years later. Architects in the 1920s and after filled this part of Los Angeles with homes designed in an array of traditional and European styles, including English Tudor, Spanish Mediterranean, Venetian Renaissance, French Normandy, Craftsman, California Bungalow, and Art Deco. At the same time, new contemporary architectural concepts began dotting the landscape throughout Los Angeles. The more geometric, visibly lighter styles drew on the new European-borne Bauhaus movement of the day but also incorporated more open floor plans with an abundance of glass to take advantage of the year-round warmth and sunlight. These parallel styles, traditional and contemporary, continue to thrive throughout today's more densely populated Hollywood Hills and greater Los Angeles basin where the imaginations and innovations of younger generations of architects and designers hasten to push the boundaries of creativity and taste. The results range from the subtle to the spectacular.

In the early part of the 20th century an adventurous breed of motion picture production companies from New York and New Jersey began migrating to Los Angeles to take advantage of the same warm climate and longer sunlit days. Throughout the roaring twenties, stage actors, writers, and directors traveled west to find work in the movies. One newcomer, for instance, was a young, single actor named Archibald Leach. He moved to Hollywood in 1931 and soon adopted his much more familiar stage name, Cary Grant (coincidentally a lifelong friend of Howard Hughes). Grant's legendary film characters in, to name a few, *Indiscreet* (with Ingrid Bergman), *An Affair to Remember* (with Deborah Kerr), *That Touch of Mink* (with Doris Day), *North by Northwest* (with Eva Marie Saint), and *Charade* (with Audrey Hepburn) cemented his persona as a romantic lead and serial bachelor.

Ever since, the movies and then television have introduced a procession of characters portraying bachelors of all stripes. Films like *Shampoo, Three Men and a Baby, Bad Boys, and The 40 Year Old Virgin*, along with popular television series such as *My Three Sons, The Courtship of Eddie's Father, Full House, Three's Company, Frasier, Two and Half Men, and Will & Grace*, have featured single men in a variety of dramatic and comedic situations. While these characters – young, mature, straight, gay, widowed, or divorced, and with or without children – have entertained us, they have also reflected and influenced our tastes. We have laughed, cried and sometimes slept through their love lives and alternately absurd and familiar circumstances usually in their fictional homes.

Hollywood and its environs impose indelible effects on its inhabitants and their lifestyles. Their lives coexist with the glamour of success and fame and the equal specter of failure and despair that make it *tinseltown*. On some level, small or grand, Hollywood's dramas and comedies, real or perceived, inform the choices, tastes, attitudes and relationships of the men who live and work in Los Angeles. Included in this aura of celebrity are not only the actors, musicians, directors, producers, and agents but also the entrepreneurs, investors, lawyers, real estate developers, plastic surgeons, fashion designers, top hairdressers, and even the accountants – all playing their part in the perpetual creation that is Hollywood. In turn, the men who choose this place to live, become influential themselves notably through their visual creativity, their sense of style, and through their patronage of art and design.

This book acknowledges bachelors – with their diverse personalities and attitudes, where one might display a diamond-studded Rolex on their wrist another wears a more discreet Patek Philippe – for their imaginative commitment to architecture and design in a climate of myriad possibilities. In tandem, this book focuses its gaze on the professionals who designed the homes their patrons afforded. The ensuing pages are filled with a selection of photographs which depict beautifully designed homes for bachelors. Accompanying each residence or project is an interview with its' respective architects and designers.

A young Cary Grant at his beach front home

While we will catch a glimpse into the private living spaces of these bachelors, some have requested to remain anonymous. Chapters divide this book by geographic regions within Los Angeles, which offers stunning locations from the hills of Hollywood and the proximity of Bel-Air to the beaches of Malibu. Beyond locale, these remarkable domains, which these men have adopted and built, contribute to the myth and reality of life in Hollywood. Their homes facilitated this record of their taste in architecture, a functional art form which has come to signify one of the vibrant and particular qualities of Southern California culture.

For longer than a decade, I have worked in Hollywood as an interior designer, furniture maker and store owner. My clients have included Hollywood actors, writers, producers, musicians, and executives – many of them bachelors. While focusing on their careers, these men have relied upon my skills and tastes as a designer. At times, they have appreciated and depended on my assistance in mentoring them through home cooking tasks, laundry techniques, and especially in staging a home for entertaining and dating. It was through these experiences that I felt compelled to compose a broader record of this perspective through the designs of other practitioners and their clients. Finally, my work with unattached men was fun and rewarding – hence this tribute to the Hollywood bachelor pads.

A mansion in Pacific Palisades

Modern architecture built into the hills

Factory-built, sustainable construction

Chapter I

VISIONS OF SAND AND WATER

Coastal Homes

"Just play. Have fun." **—Michael Jordan**

Solitude for early morning surfers

Malibu, a 27-mile strip of Pacific coastline, has lured surfers and moguls alike for decades. The beaches are public, but these days the homes along the sand serve as weekend retreats for billionaires. And, it shows. This prime beachfront property features showcase architecture from unassuming retro bungalows to austere ultra-modern monoliths all tightly squeezed together. Long the playground of movie stars, Malibu has been called home by the likes of Leonardo DiCaprio, Bill Murray, Adam Sandler, Matthew McConaughey, and Sean Penn. Before them, Malibu's Surfrider Beach became the celluloid stomping ground of the fictional movie characters Gidget and Moondoggie and alternatively, Frankie and DeeDee.

Immediately south, the city of Santa Monica features an amusement park and concerts on its main pier, attracting millions of visitors each year. Neighboring Pacific Palisades offers hillside views and the famed J. Paul Getty Museum and Romanesque villa. Continuing south along the coast Venice Beach, known for its ornate inhabitants, freely entertains beachgoers strolling its boardwalk and "muscle beach." Here the architecture – an eclectic mix of rundown Craftsman bungalows, artist studios, and contemporary three-story homes – blend together from the wide sandy beaches to the canals a few blocks inland.

In the Thirties, these were the beach cities that became the weekend hangouts for stars like Cary Grant and Clark Gable. The warm climate and a fertile culture of artists, surfers, and musicians evolved to create styles and movements unique to Los Angeles. Since the Fifties artists living in Venice and Santa Monica shaped the region from a Bohemian backwater to an important destination on the art world map. Decades later a now historic yet forever young Venice Beach would attract a new generation of leading men like Nicholas Cage, Robert Downey, Jr., and Elijah Wood. These days, properties have sky-rocketed in price but the looks are still free. For the bachelors in this chapter, life on "the endless summer" is well worth the price of admission.

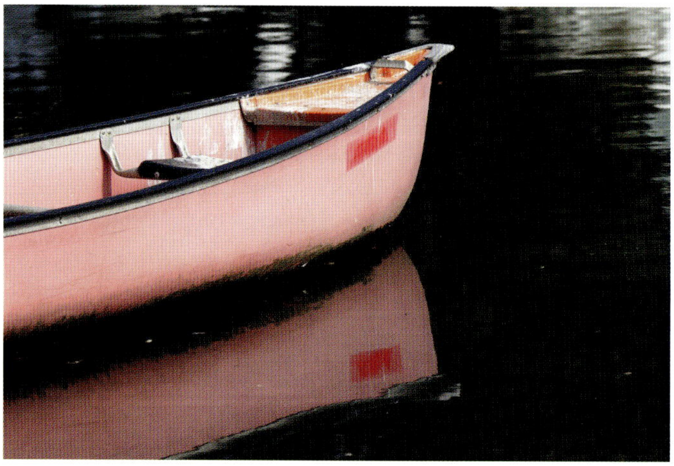

Boating is still a pastime on the Venice Canals

Lunching at a beach side café in Malibu

A view of the Santa Monica pier at night

THE REMEDY

Interview with architect Stephen Kanner

Fire destroyed the site of this original structure in the mid-1990s.

Stephen Kanner is director of internationally recognized Kanner Architects. Celebrating over 60 years of architectural design, this firm explores, develops and produces progressive syntheses of warm and timeless Modernist architecture. They create environments that are sensitive to site, sustainable, mindful of the human scale, and inventive in use of materials. This firm has garnered over three dozen design awards as well as graced the covers of numerous architectural books and magazines. Kanner, who has created a residence in Malibu for a private bachelor, tells us about his project.

I understand this residence was originally destroyed in the Malibu fires a few years back. The owner then asked you to build something completely new for him. In designing this comprehensive remodel what were your influences?

Our new design is minimal, yet has warm aesthetics inspired by Luis Barragan, the Mexican master of space and light who is known for sculptural courtyard designs. Other sources of inspiration are Greek island architecture and the simple cubist work of Irving Gil, who specialized in internal courtyards.

Operable glass walls fold and slide to open the house to the outside.

White plaster makes up the exterior of this one-story courtyard home, enhancing the contrast of the blue sky and ocean nearby.

Scenery surrounds the property and the new design allows the owner full views.

Located on a secluded crest in the Malibu hills, this home takes full advantage of the breathtaking views this area provides.

Notice the play of shapes created for the structure. Spaces intersect inside and outside the house.

You've taken cues from the natural surroundings and incorporated these elements beautifully into this home.

Our design takes full advantage of its secluded location on a crest in the Malibu hills and the breathtaking views that site provides. For example, the one-story courtyard home's white plaster exterior is enhanced by its contrast with the blue sky and nearby ocean. The stark forms are juxtaposed further with the warm interior features of mahogany floors, doors and cabinets.

Can you describe the structure?

The home's plan establishes a hierarchy of space through varying ceiling heights. Vertical space is greatest in the living room, dining room and master bedroom. Alternating room heights result in a spatial compression and expansion that references the undulating fluidity of the Pacific outside

The stark forms are juxtaposed further with the warm interior features of this kitchen including mahogany floors, doors and cabinets.

The courtyard, viewed from the master bedroom, was inspired by Luis Barragan, the Mexican master of space and light who is known for sculptural courtyard designs.

Cues from the natural surrounding were incorporated into this home's design.

Another source of inspiration for this home was Greek island architecture.

The operable glass walls that fold and slide to open the house to the outside appear to remove barriers between the resident and the horizon, providing unobstructed views of mountains and ocean. You've done a wonderful design making the most of this residence and allowing the owner to enjoy the scenery in which he is surrounded.

Unobstructed views of mountains are seen from the open bathroom.

Majestic hues of color spread across the sky at sunset.

THE SPACE BETWEEN

Interview with Kanner Architects

Kanner Architects, who created the previous home, have also designed this residence located in Malibu. Here, we discuss Kanner's work for a single man.

The residence, including the dining room, is oriented to receive maximum sunlight through the expansive windows.

This home, which essentially is two cubes linked by a staircase, counters the complexity and wildness of the rugged hills surrounding it. What were your thoughts behind this idea?

The house's extruded modernist composition is a reaction to many conditions of the project: the site's linear topography, a desire for massive window openings to take in spectacular views of the mountains immediately outside and the ocean in the distance, the need for fire resistance, and a requirement for xeriscape.

This home, which essentially is two cubes linked by a staircase, counters the complexity and remaining wilderness of the rugged hills surrounding it.

Cherry wood on both levels ties the structure's interiors.

The home's interior, as seen from the living room, is a mixture of cool and warm. One example is the cool concrete paved floors along the warm woods used in the common spaces on the main level.

From the master bedroom, the client has vistas of both the mountains and canyons with their dramatic weather changes and the ocean beyond.

This home is fire-resistant, planted with drought tolerant landscaping.

One can see amazing views from this natural light filled home.

The residence is oriented to receive maximum sunlight and all rooms have expansive windows eager to receive the rays. From the master bedroom, the client has vistas of both the mountains and canyons with their dramatic weather changes and the ocean beyond.

One would think this home would be extremely warm in the summer, but it is not.

A mere 25 feet wide, the building's lean profile provides excellent cross-ventilation of abundant sea breezes. The layered composition of the west elevation allows for large dual-glazed openings with the numerous projections to shade the glass.

A mere 25 feet wide, the building's lean profile provides excellent cross-ventilation taking advantage of abundant sea breezes.

Massive window openings take in spectacular views of mountains and the ocean in the distance.

The house's extruded modernist composition is a reaction to the site's linear topography.

The layered composition of the west elevation allows for large dual-glazed openings with the numerous projections to shade the glass.

The colors used also give a sense of coolness, yet it still feels comfortable and not too stark. Can you describe the interior color palate and materials?

The home's interior is a mixture of cool and warm. The main level, with its common spaces, has a floor of concrete pavers. The bedrooms upstairs are carpeted,. The presence of marble (white, blue and matt-black) and cherry wood on both levels unite the whole.

Set in the hills of Malibu overlooking the Pacific Ocean, this home exudes power and is unafraid to be transparent. It shows how the masters of the universe can feel at home.

One can see amazing vistas from this natural light filled home.

Set in the hills of Malibu overlooking the Pacific Ocean, this home exudes power and is unafraid to be transparent.

Interview with designer Johnna McHugh of JMID on the home of Hollywood bachelor Angus Mitchell

Interior designer Johnna McHugh, originally a ballerina with the New York City Ballet, studied interior design while living and performing in London. Today, she is an accomplished designer and art consultant. Her client, Angus Mitchell, is heir to the Paul Mitchell fortune. His well-known father built a hair-care legacy that started at a London salon where celebrities like The Beatles and Twiggy waited in line to have their locks tousled. With positive energy and compassion, Angus himself has become an international educator in the industry. Johanna talks about the Pacific Palisades home she created for Angus.

Dale Chihuly's site-specific glass sculpture, Persian Flowers, hangs in the entry.

First of all, I wanted to chat about how a female views design projects. Other women designers have said that it is different when working with a single man in that it is easier, that their client trusts their decisions and relies more on their expertise. Did you have that feeling with this project?

Definitely.

As women, we seem to have a nurturing sense when dealing with a male client. Several designers talked about being more protective of their client or helping out in his home in small ways like arranging flowers, rinsing dishes in the sink, that sort of thing. Do you have this same experience with your client?

Yes. I decorate Angus' Christmas trees, always set the table for Thanksgiving or any important dinner party he may be having.

Angus stands in front of one of one of the many pieces from his art collection.

The columns and ceilings in the entry are faux painted stone to match the existing reclaimed stone on the floor.

An oil painting is hung along the gallery walls in the upper hallway.

One of the many landscapes is displayed from Angus' collection.

An intimate landscape hangs below an antique light fixture.

What was your design plan for creating a home for Angus?

I wanted to create the feeling of an historic family owned Italian Villa inhabited by a young European aristocrat. My goal was to create interiors filled with valuable family heirlooms and a collection of serious contemporary art.

Were there any specific requests?

My client asked for interiors that would be comfortable for entertaining both large and small scale events. It also needed to be comfortable when he was alone with his two dogs, and every room needed to be dog friendly as well. This also needed to be a home in which a woman would feel comfortable. A home theatre was to be included. In addition, at the planning phase of the project we needed to leave empty walls for an art collection that didn't yet exist.

An early 20th century Samuel May pool table along with a turn-of-the-century clock provide the billiard room with function and whimsy.

Walking through the entry, I see you have a Murano light fixture. I purchase originals whenever I can find them – they're like jewels to me and can make a great statement in any room. Can you tell me about this piece and some of the other furnishings we see here in the entry, stairs and upper hall?

The entry chandelier is a 12-arm Murano style and a re-issue of an original design. The columns and ceiling are faux painted stone to match the existing reclaimed stone on the floor. The lion is a 17th century faience garden piece, and the 16th century marble bust is Italian.

Master bedrooms and bathrooms are personal spaces for a bachelor.

Angus' bedroom was created as a place for rest and contemplation. The most important piece of Angus' art collection, David Hockney's 2004 Courtyard Palace of Carlos Alhambra, was reserved for this space.

Angus is Scottish and his roots are very important to him so in the bathroom. I had two large cabinets reproduced with hand carved and gilded Scottish rams heads for use as over-counter cabinets.

Red dominates the media room, which features an Arco lamp, Fortuny drapery, and Linea sofas.

An oil painting by Tony Bevan dominates the interior of the living room.

Angus' request was that every room be comfortable and dog friendly.

Leather and ebony arm chairs along with the Paul Smith rug complete the study.

How would you describe the success of this project for Angus?

The Client is an extremely visual man. He trusted me and was able to make decisions quickly. His self-confidence allowed him to take risks and there was never a moment of wondering what others might think. With this attitude we were able to make bold choices and the result was strong and classic yet extremely unique.

A Rose Tarlow bench is seen in the upper hallway.

Angus' bedroom was created as a place for rest and contemplation.

A vignette in the entry includes an antique chair and a 16th century Italian marble bust.

Over the fireplace is a flat screen television that is concealed when not in use.

Upholstered walls and antique Chinese bed grace the Opium room.

The most important piece of Angus' art collection, David Hockney's 2004 *Courtyard Palace of Carlos Alhambra*, was reserved for this space.

Custom upholstery by Johanna compliments the bedroom retreat.

Angus Mitchell's home, an Italian-style villa, is situated in Pacific Palisades.

SIMPLE THINGS

Interview with designer Melinda Gray of GRAYmatter

An expansive stairway leads to the second floor.

A useful design element in Southern California, the living room opens to the outside.

Melinda Gray is an architect for GRAYmatter, a firm specializing in alternative design, technologies, materials, and forms. These questions are about her work and her Anonymous Bachelor who lives in Santa Monica.

I'd like to first ask what inspired you to study architecture?

I always was interested in making space and form with whatever I could get my hands on, even as a child. Whether it was snow, ice, junk, whatever was available.

I can relate. As children, I competed with my brothers in the extreme sport of snow sculpting – igloos, snow towers, snow forts – it was never a dull moment as a kid. For your client in Santa Monica, what was the design criteria and what opportunities did the property have for you to be creative?

We wanted to open up to the outdoors and create an indoor-outdoor life. The house sits on a site surrounded by an upslope that we used to create our own world. The sloping wall onto which the entire house orients combines a fireplace, fountain and cooking area drawing the inside to the out.

With constant warmth and few mosquitoes, outdoor living is enjoyed year round.

Comfortable seating is mandatory in this outdoor living space.

North views look into the canyon.

Custom pieces were created for the master bedroom which looks toward a courtyard.

A living room opening to the outside is a wonderful design element to incorporate into a residence in southern California. Was this an idea that you introduced to the client or collaboration?

It was me…I always think this way and design every house with this feature, as this is how we live here. We don't have mosquitoes or bugs, and it's warm enough to be outside all the time.

The kitchen appears to be quite functional as well as light filled and open. Were there any 'green' or recycled materials used in construction?

The concept was to have a kitchen everyone can hang out in, with plenty of room to cook, prepare, eat, etc. We used recycled wood beams for the stairs (made of wood chips) since we were having trouble finding solid wood that size. We took the idea further and made the kitchen island of the same material.

The concept was to have a kitchen where everyone can hang out and have plenty of room to cook.

The master bedroom suite you created also opens up to the elements. Whose idea was it to have this all open?

Actually, it was my (a woman) who came up with the concept of having everything open, even the clothes storage, kind of like living in a boutique, where you can see all the clothes at a glance, without having to open up drawers or doors. I had been designing a few boutiques at the time and though I would like to be able to see all the clothes at a glance, so I tried it with Tom. The one issue we had was getting his housekeeper to fold as neatly as the boutique sales people do.

Recycled wood beams were used for the stairs and the kitchen island.

Custom made dressing cabinetry was incorporated into the master suite.

OH WHAT A NIGHT

Interview with Architect Steven Ehrlich

This house, in the heart of Venice Beach, offers a smart variation on courtyard living.

This exterior courtyard entry is a sensible solution to maximizing privacy and outdoor enjoyment in an urban setting.

Internationally recognized Ehrlich Architect's approach to design extends the traditions of architectural innovation and the fusion of technology with cultural and environmental sensitivity. Here Steven Ehrlich discusses his work and the home he designed a few steps from Venice Beach for his client, a single man.

Looking at the project you created for your client, how would you describe it?

This house, in the heart of Venice Beach, represents another variation on courtyard living as a sensible solution to maximizing privacy and outdoor enjoyment in an urban setting. The principal living areas are two-story painted stucco boxes separated by a garden; with concrete steps descending from the rear space, which is built at a higher level, the courtyard becomes a verdant amphitheatre. Glass roll-up doors facing the interior courtyard and the front entrance court allow unimpeded views through the ground floor, and when opened transform the house into an airy pavilion.

Venice is very dense and property is set at a premium. How did you address this?

For the 3,600 square foot Residence, the design provides a cohesive plan that is pulled apart to leave an internal tranquil courtyard at its center. In plan, the building consists of two volumes at each end of the lot, linked by a service spine on the east and the central courtyard complete with a reflecting pool.

Most of the local residences consists of single bedroom beach houses from the 1940s and newer apartment super-blocks that force residents to enjoy the coastal weather from cramped, dark balconies or through small side windows. The structure that you erected for your client reflects a more tranquil and open environment, which is both refreshing and innovative for this neighborhood.

Glass roll-up doors facing the interior courtyard and the front entrance court allow for uninterrupted views through the living room.

A private rooftop, complete with fireplace, provides a tranquil and refreshing area for entertaining.

The building consists of two volumes at each end of the lot, linked by a service spine.

The 3,600-square-foot residence includes this large master bath with its own view

DO IT TO IT

Interview with Living Homes Steve Glen on his own Hollywood bachelor home

Architect Ray Kappe, known for his fine craftsmanship and special attention to details, designed this modern home that was pre-fabricated off site.

Living Homes is a firm that creates and builds sustainable and efficient homes. Their homes, designed by top architects, feature modern designs and are constructed in factories using natural non-toxic materials and energy efficiency. One of the first of these homes, situated in Santa Monica, is owned by bachelor and CEO of this company, Steve Glen.

The house consists of 70% insulated glass and the rest of the structure is energy-efficient using high performance insulation made from 100% recycled denim fabric.

Steve, looking at the interior entry one is struck by the interplay of layers, textures and materials.

Yes, Ray Kappe, one of my favorite architects, designed this home. He is known for his fine craftsmanship and special attention to details.

This is an open floor plan, tell me about the living room area.

There is a large indoor garden that has special plants used for creating oxygen while filtering contaminates in the air. The sofa is recycled from my old home and the Eames chair is made of sustainable rosewood.

Steve's open floor plan shows an interplay of layers, textures and materials.

The Eames lounge in the living area is made of sustainable rosewood.

The kitchen counter is Paperstone, made of recycled newsprint sealed with Linseed oil. The under-sink food composter creates pellets that are used to feed the plants.

The large indoor garden contains special plants used for creating oxygen while filtering contaminants in the air.

Your home has a sense of warmth with its use of organic materials and there is natural light everywhere from the glass. But, because there is so much glass throughout this house, does the interior get too warm in the summer?

The house is 70% insulated glass and the rest of the house is energy efficient because we incorporated high performance insulation, which is made from 100% recycled denim fabric.

What other efficiencies does the house have?

The fireplace burns denatured alcohol and creates lots of heat but no smoke.

The heater is a radiant heat system and the water in it is heated from solar collectors installed on the roof.

Tell me about the exterior landscaping around the house?

The exterior is planted with native and drought tolerant plants, and we've installed a gray water system recycling water from the sink, washing machine and shower.

I remember when I was in college years ago, we talked of the idea of grey water systems but they were not allowed yet, which I thought was a shame since they could save so much water waste. Considering the issues of this planet we face today, we need to recycle as much as possible. You have an outdoor spa, how is that powered?

The waterfall and my Jacuzzi are powered by PV's.

Its great to see how PV's ("photovoltaic", defined as the application of solar cells used to convert sunlight directly into electricity) have taken off in the last ten years in California.

I see you use a lot of wood in the interior of the house. The ceilings and walls appear to be Cedar, what can you say about this?

The wood is certified by the Forest Stewardship Council which insures the sustainable growth and practices from the nurseries.

The home, including this master bedroom, is heated with a radiant heat system, in which water is heated from solar collectors installed on the roof.

Non-toxic materials and low VOC paints were used in the master bedroom.

I assume the paints and stains used throughout are organic?

Yes, we use low VOC's, Volatile organic compounds.

And, tell me what cool stuff you have going on in your kitchen.

The kitchen counter is Paperstone, made of recycled newsprint and sealed with linseed oil. Under the sink is a food compost bin, which creates pellets that are used to feed the plants.

What can you say about living here?

Happy & Healthy!

The exterior is planted with native and drought tolerant plants. The water comes from a gray water system which recycles water from the sink, washing machine, and shower.

Wood installed throughout the home and bathroom is certified by the Forest Stewardship Council which insures the sustainable growth practices from the nurseries.

Interview with Architect Michael Sant on Home of Hollywood Bachelor, Ray Azoulay

Azouley's home uniquely blurs the line between home and studio, ideal for a bachelor at play.

Michael Sant, principal of Sant Architects, designed and built a 3 story mixed use structure in Venice. The building was designed to interweave the public and private spaces and link the residences to the street. Sant created the space for Obsolete Gallery owner Ray Azoulay.

The back wall in the bedroom is paneled in corrugated English basswood, salvaged from last summer's renovation of Lincoln Center's Alice Tully Hall.

The living area is filled with vintage furnishings and art from Ray's collection.

The two-story loft that Azoulay lives in is a on a half bloc of a busy area of Venice. What have you done to create a quiet environment for the inhabitants?

Though the street life on Abbot Kinney Boulevard is lively, the development's residential portion, which occupies the top two stories, "is tranquil with a sense of repose". Split into two masses by a 15-foot-wide garden courtyard, the three-story structure is further broken up by four stairwells carved deep into the facades.

Deferring to your vision, Azoulay took a fixed and minimalist approach to furnishing his residence.

Yes, although the assortment of pieces within his space are no less unusual than what he has in his shop.

Beside the sofa stands Vico Magistretti's globular glass floor lamp.

Ray's loft includes an open dining area, adorned with an assortment of pieces from Azouley's shop.

Art adorns this corner of the loft.

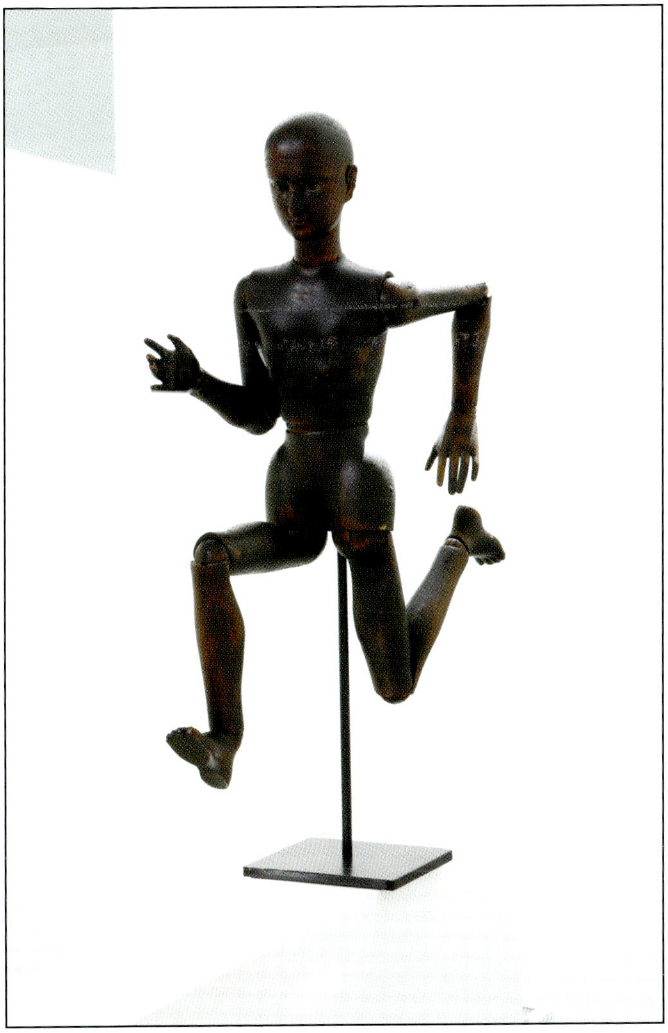

A whimsical art model from Ray's collection.

What was cosmetically done to Azoulay's space?

We exposed its bow-truss ceiling, unearthed the concrete floor beneath carpet, and then his diverse pieces were brought in for display.

The floors are gray polished concrete flooring and the walls are painted white.

Yes, I wanted to keep it monochromatic.

Azouley's art collection sets the tone in his loft.

Other pieces are displayed with harmony in the art-filled house.

The bathroom design reflects a masculine and minimalist style.

Artwork is tucked in a corner of the kitchen.

The master bedroom has a mix of old and new and the room feels like something you would find in a New York loft. What are some of the furnishings?

The caramel leather sofa, circa 1930 and beside it is a Vico Magistretti's globular glass floor lamp. Philippe Allaeys's oak bed is from 2001. A sidewall is paneled in corrugated English basswood, salvaged from last summer's renovation of Lincoln Center's Alice Tully Hall.

This loft resembles a curatorial laboratory done with Gothic touches. Azouley's place, uniquely blurs the line between home and studio, ideal for a bachelor at play.

The loft's stairwell appears tranquil with a sense of repose.

The building was designed to interweave public and private spaces.

The three-story structure is further broken up by four stairwells carved deep into the facades.

The two-story loft that Azoulay lives in occupies a half bloc of a busy area of Venice.

Chapter 2

PALM TREES, HEDGES & BLING

Beverly Hills & Bel Air Areas

"*There's no place like home.*" —**Barry Bonds**

Trees line the residential streets in Beverly Hills.

One of the shops of Rodeo Drive.

Television shows like *Beverly Hills 90210* and decades earlier the *Beverly Hillbillies* introduced generations of Americans to Beverly Hills – home to mansions, movie stars, spoiled children, and Rodeo Drive, where high-end boutiques (Chanel, Dior, Giorgio, Cartier and the like) sell toys and baubles for the well-heeled. A century earlier, farmers tilled the fields of Beverly Hills for lima beans.

A limo cruises along in Beverly Hills.

Neighboring Beverly Hills is Bel-Air. Together these two communities contain some of the most expensive mansions in the world. Men who have called this home include Jerry Seinfeld, Paul McCartney, George Lucas and Jay Leno. This chapter offers an amazing glimpse into the architecture and design of homes that continue to shape the landscape of this area.

Indiginous flora blooms year-round in Bel-Aire.

Interview with architect Duncan Nicholson on the home of Hollywood bachelor James Goldstein

Architect John Lautner once said, "this structure is a cave whose opening points out toward the Los Angeles basin and the Pacific Ocean to the horizon line beyond."

Duncan Nicholson, who once worked for renowned architect John Lautner, believes that architecture is the formation of space built from an idea. His eponymous firm, Duncan Nicholson Architect, focuses its practice on new concepts and the latest incantations. In addition, since Lautner's death in 1994, Duncan has led the remodel and restoration of a 1963 Lautner design owned by the enigmatic James Goldstein.

What is known about Jim Goldstein is his flamboyant yet informed taste in couture fashion, modern architecture, contemporary art, and NBA basketball. He lives in what many consider a modern masterpiece situated on a cliff in the Benedict Canyon area above Beverly Hills.

The home offers 180 degrees of panoramic views of the night sky.

Jim's commitment to Lautner also extended to his professional life through his Century City office interiors, which he commissioned Lautner to design. Around 2005, Jim moved out, and the Los Angeles Cultural Heritage Commission conferred Historic-Cultural Monument status on the office to preserve the sole remaining commercial work designed by Lautner in pristine condition. As a result, the Los Angeles County Museum of Art will place the Goldstein office on permanent display.

An apprentice of Frank Lloyd Wright before striking out on his own, Lautner practiced architecture in Los Angeles from 1939 until his death. One of his greatest designs, a residence in Los Angeles commonly known as the Chemosphere, stands precariously on a single support. It has appeared in major motion pictures as have other Lautner designs, including the Elrod House in Palm Springs, which was prominently featured in the James Bond film, *Diamonds Are Forever*. Although not quite a household name, among Mid-Century cognoscenti an original built design by the architect is described in their lexicon simply as a "Lautner."

Lautner, the man, completed the Sheats/Goldstein residence in 1963 and was commissioned in 1989 by Jim to remodel his acquisition. Duncan Nicholson took over the project after Lautner passed away.

Duncan talks about his work on Jim's ... Lautner.

The materials of stone, steel and wood converge to form the entertainment area.

John Lautner was a disciple of Frank Lloyd Wright, which becomes apparent when looking at some of the Usonian elements of Jim's house.

The Spartan office balances form and simplicity in a complex digital world.

The living area fills with light during the day.

John Lautner was a student of Frank Lloyd Wright, which is apparent when looking at some of the elements of Jim's house. The assemblage of geometric triangles of wood and glass is formed in such a way that it innately coexists with its natural surroundings.

The Sheats/Goldstein Structure, as John Lautner did say, is a cave who's opening points out toward the Los Angeles basin and the Pacific Ocean to the horizon line beyond.

The 180 degrees of panoramic views are amazing. When you are inside, you still feel like you are part of the outside yet safe from the outdoor elements.

It is the imposing coffered reinforced roof structure overhead with the frameless glass enveloping the space that provides the quality of freedom and the security desired.

I know changes were made after Jim took ownership of this space.

Originally designed for a family, Lautner and Jim Goldstein completely rethought the original and then remade it in Mr. Goldstein's image. This is not only a testament to the flexible quality of Lautner's architectural approach with his clients but also to the malleability of his buildings which he always said were spaces that made one feel "FREE!" How else for the space to be described as free than for it to be able to be reworked into another seamless space perfectly suited to an individual rather than a large family?

The assemblage of geometric triangles of wood and glass appears to innately coexist with its natural surroundings.

Natural surroundings envelope the structure.

The water, koi and plant life complement in free-form to Launter's geometries.

The ongoing restoration includes the addition of a pool.

What has your role been in this project since you took it over?

My office tries to do everything that I learned from John. It is a fantastic job and we get to design everything! I have designed a new office on site for Jim Goldstein, a nightclub, a new swimming pool, furniture, even ashtrays. You name it, we get to do it.

Artist Charlie Fine referred me to Jim and said he is a really great guy. How has it been working with Jim?

Mr. Goldstein is a fantastic client, always full of ideas so the back and forth energy and vibrancy keeps plowing the design forward into the future. If we don't think it's beautiful it isn't going to happen. The job is a dream and for me, one of the great rewards of it, is being allowed stand in these inspired spaces John designed. They are profoundly uplifting, always alive and always beautiful.

Originally designed for a family, Lautner and Jim Goldstein completely rethought the original home and then remade it in Mr. Goldstein's image.

IRREPLACEABLE

Interview with Architects Steven Shortridge and Barbara Callas on the home of Hollywood bachelor Glen Berenbeim

Steven Shortridge and Barbara Callas, once senior associates with the parent firm of Franklin D. Israel Design Associates, have years of experience working on design and construction for influential projects. Published in major magazines, their homes reflect their high standards of design excellence. Their client, Glen Berenbeim, is a writer and producer living in Benedict Canyon.

A sequential progression of privacy and quietness, transparency and solidity, moving from a busy street to a minimally landscaped and gated entry courtyard define the approach to the entrance.

The black plaster fireplaces and stainless fireboxes provide stylistic continuity throughout the house and a visual link between the fire and water elements.

Glen's home is intelligent design. Can you describe the structure in relation to its site and the street?

The U-shaped house is perched on a level platform between a descending slope to the street and a steep amphitheater-like canyon rising in the back of the house, creating a sense of privacy from other homes in the canyon.

The entry leading to the house has a great sense of solitude and balance.

A sequential progression of privacy and quietness, transparency and solidity, moving from a busy street to a minimally landscaped and gated entry courtyard define the approach to the entrance.

White plastered courtyard walls reminiscent of the house, one of which traverses the length of the house and punctuated by a steel louvered screen opening, expand the sense of privacy from the street. This wall marks the front of the house from the driveway below and forms an entry courtyard visible from the main living area through the floor-to-ceiling glass.

A tile water feature in the serene courtyards leads to a 7-foot-wide wooden entry door.

The natural materials and colors emulate the natural environment outside.

Natural light fills the home and the interiors play well with the exterior.

Through a series of spatial transformations, the interior of the house is able to engage exterior spaces in large expanses of glass and sliding doors. Although the U-shaped plan of the house remained, the plan and character was significantly transformed to take advantage of light, space, and the canyon setting. A stainless steel spout punctuates one end of the fountain, while the other end of the fireplace is punctuated by a stainless steel and sand filled firebox, both of which are visible when in the living room.

The skylights and ceilings contribute to the success of the house and bring cohesiveness throughout.

The restored tongue and groove vaulted ceiling in the living room is bisected by a large primer-colored steel beam and terminated by a Douglass fir cabinet, which doubles as a screen to the private areas of the house. These elements create a flow within the cooler shell, providing a thematic link from space to space.

The restored tongue and groove vaulted ceiling in the living room is bisected by a large primer-colored steel beam and terminated by a Douglass fir cabinet, which doubles as a screen to the private areas of the house. These elements create a glow within the cooler shell, providing a thematic link from space to space.

The continuity of materials creates a tone to the house that is alternately cool and warm, but coexists within a larger canvas.

Architectural elements of structure, space, material, and light are incorporated into Glen Berenbeim's bedroom.

Comfortable seating completes the master bedroom suite.

PUT IT ON ME

Interview with Architect Dean Larkin

Architect Dean Larkin, a native of LA, grew up among the unique climate and lifestyle of Southern California. His projects, including celebrity homes (Lily Tomlin, Jane Wagner and Tom & Shelby Arnold) span across major cities within the U.S. and have been published in major newspapers and home magazines. His work focuses on maximizing the intrinsic potential of each setting and lifestyle needs of his clients. Dean talks about his work for a single man who lives in Beverly Hills.

Dean, I am always curious, so I like to ask the question: what got you thinking of becoming an architect?

I was one of those goofy kids always destined to be an architect. When I was 16 during the summer months off from school I would drop my dad off at work and armed with a "Homes for Sale" magazine, I would hit all the model homes I could before I had to pick him up later that day.

The new master suite enjoys handsome views of the back yard and pool, while seamlessly blending with the existing architecture.

That's funny. I did model home design years ago in the start of my career and found it vexing to create a space for an imaginary home owner. I preferred to collaborate with a real person to incorporate his personality into a space.

Many architects talk about the mentors they are influenced by, who were yours?

As a Native of Southern California I can't help but be influenced by the works of Neutra, Wright (both father and son), Schindler, Paul Williams, and Lautner. I am also influenced by the architecture of film and TV.

I grew up in the Midwest and my school was named Frank Lloyd Wright (and many of his homes were in our region) so I too, was captivated by Wright. I agree with your choice of LA architects and feel that this city is more interesting because of them.

When starting to create a home for our clients, they usually discuss their desires and wishes. What was your client's desire?

The client wanted to reinvent the house with a "spa-like" feel.

Can you tell me about what changes you made to this house?

This was an outdated Beverly Hills house so I updated it and expanded the structure to include a new master suite, entry foyer and garage.

The client wanted to reinvent the house with a "spa like" feel. Decorative niches provide an accent to the adjacent two-way fireplace in the great room.

The new entry foyer is the 'heart' of the addition, providing a link between the existing house and the new structure.

This was an outdated Beverly Hills house that was expanded to include a new master suite, entry foyer and garage.

As a unifying design motif, the circle is seen throughout the home from the entry, courtyard and into the master bath.

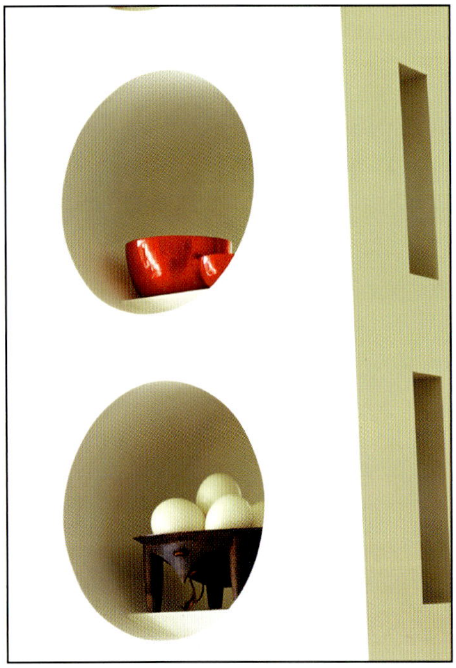

Storage details, shown as circular cubbies, were created in the kitchen.

For the outside, new textured concrete block walls were added to update the front elevation, thereby layering the façade with natural materials to emphasize the new entry.

The house seems to combine the indoor with the outdoor spaces by incorporating a harmonious flow throughout the home. Can you give examples of how you achieved this?

For example, the new master suite enjoys handsome views of the back yard and pool, while seamlessly blending with the existing architecture. For the outside, new textured concrete block walls were added to update the front elevation - layering the façade with natural materials emphasizing the new entry. Bringing the outside in, throughout the house, the circle form was introduced. This both complements and softens the rigid geometries of the wall. As a unifying design motif, the circle is seen throughout the home from the entry, courtyard and into the master bath.

You did a good job! This home seems natural and emphasizes light, movement and beauty.

The new master bath extends the design ideas of the house into a round room featuring back-to-back sinks floating in the center and lit by a skylight above.

View from the rear yard showing the existing house on the right and the new master suite on the left. All major rooms of the house were reconfigured and altered to open onto the rear yard and the view.

Interview with Architect Stanley Anderson of MRY on the home of real estate visionary Rob Maguire

Twilight reflects into the home through the red entry doors.

Moore Ruble Yudell, MRY, is a widely acclaimed international design firm with an exceptional body of work that is embedded in a profound commitment to humanistic architecture. Their interior design project featured here is a classic mid century modern house owned by real estate mogul Rob Maguire. Complete with its own vineyard and private wine label (Rascal Robbie), this Bel- Air estate personifies California living at its best. Stanley Anderson, head of the interior design team at MRY, talks with me about his work and their project.

Stanley, what inspired you to study architectural design?

I was always interested in design since I was a child. I became a licensed architect, but have almost always practiced Interior Architecture. Working closely with clients with the interior elements that they come into contact with is what I am most interested.

Where would you take someone to show them the perfect LA place?

I always take visitors to Venice. Between the unique characters on the boardwalk, the expressive architecture of the various beach houses, and the beach itself, I think Venice is the quintessential LA experience.

How would you summarize the overall design criteria for this project?

The house is a classic mid century modern house by A. Quincy Jones, renovated by Fred Fisher Partners with new Pool house and Guesthouse additions by FFP. The house renovation had been completed for a couple of years with just enough pieces of furniture that the owner had collected or used in other houses he had lived. Our goal was to complete the interiors: furnishings, rugs, drapery, &accessories throughout to warm up the spaces a bit and to make the family room and bedroom more comfortable. The envelope of the house is very clean and contemporary. We combined additional antiques and modern pieces throughout to create this balance that works well in that setting.

Vivid colors were selected throughout the house to anchor each room and provide a conversation between the axial fireplaces seen from various vantage points throughout the house.

MRY selected an expansive Poliform sectional for the living room that gave a quiet, relaxed space for the extended family to lounge underneath the artwork by Frank Stella.

Offering views of the Getty Center and the Pacific Ocean, the primary-color accented kitchen is the heart of the home.

Custom red and yellow fiberglass panels (used to hide an outdoor shower and dressing area), along with a crushed blue glass roof top complete this Mies- and Philip Johnson-inspired house.

There is a link between all of the custom rugs that were placed throughout the home. They vary in texture from thick 2" high pile wool rugs in the master bedroom to silk shag rugs in the livingroom.

An intimate seating group is arranged by the fireplace.

A John McCracken wall piece hangs on the opposite wall of the living room.

One can't help but first notice the saturation of red architectural objects. Color, as you know, is an important element and your all white palette combined with bold statements of red is an exciting concept to the human eye. Was this your idea or the client's, and what was the thought behind this?

Our client's favorite color is red. It's a wonderful accent appropriate in this setting and to the aesthetic needs of the client.

I have a great admiration for anyone who is adventurous enough to collect contemporary art. Mr. Maguire's reputation as a patron is commendable and certainly arouses my own personal artistic passions and questions. In the living room seeing the Frank Stella, I am reminded of the Stella that Maguire commissioned in 1990 for his Gas Company tower. It was a 35,000 square foot mural, an incredible undertaking and the largest painted outdoor mural in the world at that time. For his own piece we see here in his home, it appears to be from the early 90s from Stella's Moby Dick Series. Did you work the room around this piece?

We definitely took inspiration from this piece. The red shag rug has a loop that is very chaotic with lots of movement, like the artwork.

The Maguire home is such a wonderful environment the moment you step onto the property. You've achieved such a minimal, artful and spiritual sense through out this space.

Outside, Robert Graham's sculptures grace the surrounding elements

This classic Bel-Air estate, complete with its own vineyard, personifies California living at its best.

CH-CHECK IT OUT

Interview with Architects John Enright and Margaret Griffin

The sloping ceiling, reflective surfaces of the floor and ceiling, and the play of light and shadow make the new open space dynamic and full of energy.

John Enright and Margaret Griffin, partners of Griffin Enright Architects, believe there is true value in the "art" of architecture and construction. Educators as well as recipients of numerous design awards, John and Margaret maintain a strong presence in both the academic and professional design worlds. Here, they discuss their work and their client, a bachelor who lives in the Benedict Canyon area of Beverly Hills.

The home you have created for your client, like so many others in Los Angeles, takes advantage of the year- round outdoor living that we are so fortunate to have. How do you incorporate this into your work philosophy?

Although we work on projects of varying scales, budgets and programs, our comprehensive approach to design remains constant: it depends on a simultaneous blurring and exploitation of distinctions between inside/outside, built form/landscape, site/urban context and theory/practice. Whenever possible, we try to underscore connections with the surrounding landscape either by reinforcing an existing condition or creating a new one that allows the architecture and landscape to be experienced in unique ways.

What were your client's wishes and the overall design scope for this project?

For the extensive renovation of this 2600- square- foot mid-century house on a hillside site in Los Angeles, our client requested nothing short of a total transformation. His desire to make the house more true to the spirit of its modernist origins included bringing in more natural light and exploiting and extending the stunning views of the canyon setting and its indigenous wildlife, accentuating the relationship between interior and exterior.

To give visual interest to the floor, existing Mexican tiles were removed and concrete underneath was finished with an epoxy resin that has a reflective, almost liquid quality.

The interior's open floorplan possesses a fluid sense of movement.

Opening up the home allowed for an extension of the stunning views of the canyon setting and its indigenous wildlife.

The ceiling, an often-neglected space in interiors, became a significant component of the overall design.

This home was created, like so many others in Los Angeles, to take advantage of year-round outdoor living.

The interior is very open and has a sense of movement but also a great feeling of warmth and texture. How did you achieve this?

On the interior, we demolished nearly all of the existing finishes and eliminated four interior walls to create open, airy, light-infused public spaces. Within the new loft-like space, discrete functional areas are defined through changes in the ceiling, placement of furniture, custom-designed built-ins and lighting. For example, we designed a custom piece made of wood supported by steel columns that appears to float between the living area and den, functioning as both bookcase and room divider. Similarly, a custom cherry-veneered and stainless steel island defines the kitchen.

The ceiling exemplifies a perfect example of form, function and light.

The ceiling, an often-neglected space in interiors, became a significant component of our overall design. We designed it to slope from 7 feet on one side to 11 feet on the other with a plywood panel system housing seemingly randomly placed track light fixtures. This system is punctuated by the intersection of two light boxes and a skylight. The light boxes are composed of resin panels with imbedded sea grass, creating a soft, glowing, filtered lighting effect. Scattered distribution of sea grass in the resin panels complements the hard edges of the ceiling. The light boxes are oriented to provide visual connections to the entry and the back yard. In an analogous fashion, the long, narrow skylight is positioned to mirror the main circulation of the house, casting striking patterns of shadows across the walls, furniture and floor.

The desire to make the house more true to the spirit of its modernist origins included bringing in more natural light.

All the existing finishes were eliminated and new materials were installed to reflect a space that is open and airy.

This 2600-square-foot, Mid-century house sits on a hillside site.

How would you describe the success of this project?

We were able to completely transform the house within a modest budget and connect the interior space with the existing landscape in a new open manner. While we did not add onto the house, the experience of the house now appears to be much larger.

A stucco wall was replaced with a 50-foot-wide wall of glass at the rear façade, opening the house to the landscape and pool.

AS GOOD AS I ONCE WAS

Interview with architect Aaron Torrance

Mid-century and Case Study restoration specialist, architect Aaron Torrence, has been sensitively rehabbing a mid century home under the watchful eyes of the city's Office of Historic Resources and the Getty Research Institute. First named the Pasinetti House, it was designed as a Case Study house by Haralamb Georgescu, a notable Romanian modernist architect. The current owner, a single man, purchased the Pasinetti House and thereby saved it from demolition in 2007. Aaron, owner of Design Plus Construction (d+Con), talks about this work.

This house has commanding views of the mountains and the distant ocean and it was first published in the January 1959 issue of Arts & Architecture magazine. Can you describe the site it sits on?

The site is along the edge of a canyon, the ground dropping sharply away from the curving street.

What were your client's wishes for this house?

My client, who is a single man, wanted a place to entertain large informal groups of people, as well as a space he could quietly write and work in.

A private study occupies the upper level. When renovation took place, Aaron utilized original construction documents to reconstruct without major disruption to the building.

The new kitchen was redesigned to take advantage of contemporary living.

The kitchen and dining areas, on the first level, open to the living room.

Understanding that you wanted to keep the integrity of the original house but also wanted to give your client upgrades, what was your plan?

Although the new owner wanted to update the house with kitchen and bathroom upgrades, he also wanted to respect the original design elements of the house. Working closely with the owner, I carefully reviewed the existing design elements and developed a new layout for the upstairs master suite and created a new kitchen and dining area, as well as a newly conceived guest bedroom that doubles as a media room - all on the lower level.

What changes were made to open up this home to more views?

In the original design the master bedroom as accessed directly off the entry door and its bathroom was set to the corner of the room - effectively the only views for the master bedroom was through a window facing the street. The new design changed the layout to provide for a sliding door off the upstairs office and opening the bathroom area to the bedroom. The master bathroom features a shower with floor-to-ceiling glass windows that command impressive views of the canyons beyond. Privacy glass at the exterior windows can turn clear to opaque at the switch of a button.

While respecting the original design elements of the house, a new kitchen and dining area were created.

The bachelor who lives here wanted a place to entertain large informal groups of people as well as a space in which he could quietly write and work.

What did you enjoy most about this project?

The best part about this project was being able to research through the original architect's sketches and drawing and photos of the house to figure out the design and construction of the building. It's rare that a 50-year old house has remained completely intact and without major modifications.

Working closely with the owner, Aaron carefully reviewed the existing design elements and developed a new layout for the master bathroom.

The owner's master retreat includes an updated bath.

The plan was developed around the large two-story high living room which can be expanded by opening the sliding doors to include the 20-foot by 20-foot outdoor deck terrace.

First published in the January 1959 issue of *Arts & Architecture* magazine, this house has commanding views of the mountains and ocean in the distance.

SHOW ME WHAT YOU GOT

Interview with architects Leo Marmol and Ron Radziner on the home of art collector Eugenio Lopez

Classic arworks, by Donald Judd on the left and Cy Twombly on the right, dramatize the foyer.

Marmol Radziner + Associates, one of the most visible and successful design-build firms in the country, are known for their ability to redefine the indoor-outdoor California lifestyle. Architects Leo Marmol and Ron Radziner, recipients of numerous design awards, are committed to creating beautiful and lasting structures which realize the necessities and dreams of their clients.

Eugenio López, the young heir to his family's fruit juice fortune, is known as a powerhouse in the art world. His Beverly Hills home, originally built by Wayne McAllister in 1957, has been reinterpreted by Marmol Radziner's team to house one of his ever-changing art collections. The mandate from the client was to preserve the spirit and character of the house while updating the finishes and redesigning the layout to accommodate his extensive art collection.

A tongue and groove ceiling, originally above the front entrance, now extends through the threshold to the foyer.

I had read a reference you made about taking a legendary architect, Albert Frey out to lunch and affectionately talked about the meal Albert ordered (which consisted solely of apple pie and chocolate ice cream). It reminded me of when I had lunch at the Arizona Biltmore with the son of Warren McArthur (his father originally built that hotel) and all he had for his meal was a decadent dessert as well. That idea, of someone ditching protocol to follow their true cravings, is what I thought of when I first walked through the Lopez home a few years ago. I was so titillated with his space that I felt like I was walking right into the desert.

Mid century architects, such as Albert Frey and Wayne McAllister, were design innovators and greatly contributed to the character of Southern California. Looking at the Lopez house, can you briefly state what your overall plan was for this structure?

Architectural features were replaced to create a more consistent style throughout a home devoted to a collection of post-war contemporary art.

The defining features of the home were the gabled ceilings, sloping rooflines and Palos Verdes stone walls. Using these motifs, we replaced awkward architectural features to create a more architecturally consistent and cohesive home. A hipped roof over the west wing was removed and replaced with a sloped roof echoing the other rooflines. A cabana addition on the west terrace was removed, opening up the house to views of Century City. A canopy along the living room façade was removed thereby creating a continuous ceiling plane connecting the interior and exterior spaces and aligning the soffit heights. A tongue and groove ceiling, originally above the front entrance, now extends through the threshold to the foyer.

A canopy along the living room façade was removed thereby creating a continuous ceiling plane connecting the interior and exterior spaces and aligning the soffit heights.

Other material choices, as seen in the study, include rift white oak flooring and casework.

The master bedroom suite now opens to views of Century City. A painting by Ed Rusche hovers over the headboard.

The master bathroom was relocated to the far end of the suite, projecting views in the adjacent garden and pool.

What was done to make this more entertainment friendly?

Interior rooms were enlarged and reconfigured to open up the space and bring in natural light. To improve circulation among the entertainment areas, the kitchen was shifted to adjoin a media room and a side terrace, which serves as an exterior dining room. With the master bedroom suite opening to the newly created views of Century City, the master bathroom was relocated to the far end of the suite, projecting views in the adjacent garden and pool.

Photographer Julius Shulman, who has been photographing structures in Los Angeles for over sixty years, was talking with me about the changes in the landscape throughout the last century. He commented about how many original mid century structures he has seen change hands and were subjected to being renovated- some well done, some not. The Lopez residence has, of course, demonstrated itself to being a marvelous example of form, functionality, and respect for its original beginnings.

Chapter 3

PANORAMA OF THE CITY

"All in all is all we are." **— Kurt Cobain**

Nighttime views of the city from the hills.

In the early years of Hollywood, the hills above were populated with oak trees, holly bushes, and poppies. Through the decades this stunning landscape has enticed homeowners and builders to craft houses ranging from French Normandy, Tudor, Mediterranean, and Mid-century modern to contemporary architecture. A high concentration of celebrities—Justin Timberlake, Leonardo DiCaprio, Keanu Reeves, and Ryan Phillipe—and entertainment moguls have resided here to soak in amazing views of the canyons and skylines while escaping the grind of the vast city.

Driving into West Hollywood.

Enjoying the open spaces of the Hollywood Hills.

Homes dot the hills to offer views of the city.

This chapter features homes situated in the Hollywood Hills and neighboring West Hollywood. These areas include Laurel Canyon and the Sunset Strip. Once known for its 1960s "hippie" music scene with legendary clubs like the Whisky A-Go-Go and The Roxy, the night life here still parties on.

Interview with architect Zolton Pali, of SPFA, on the home of Hollywood bachelor Jeff Beuth

This home is architectural perfection with its clean lines, open spaces and its relationship to the outdoors.

Zoltan E. Pali, along with Judit M. Fekete, founded the SPF architectural firm. They specialize in clients and projects that require a high level of design sensitivity, technical expertise, and hands-on principal involvement. Awarded *Architecture Magazine's* Home of the Year Award in 2003, their projects have included the 300,000 square foot Getty Villa Museum.

Client Jeff Beuth, President of City Corp Ventures, embraces Los Angeles hilltop living in his SPF designed home. Located within the so-called Bird Streets of the West Hollywood Hills, this 9,200 square foot three story residence was a 2005 winner of the CCAIA Merit Award. Jeff's residence is an entertainment haven with posh amenities that include a ballroom, screening room, billiards room and glass-walled pool.

Zoltan Pali answered the following questions.

A pair of custom sofas upholstered in pale-gray felt are flanked by a massive limestone block and magnificent views of Los Angeles.

As an architect, I'd first like to ask you what inspires or influences your work?

I must say the works of the Modern European Masters have always inspired us, and interestingly enough some of those masters were influenced by the modernist movement here in Los Angeles.

Custom full-height, ebonized-veneered cabinetry and lower cabinets clad in aluminum define the kitchen.

For access to the outdoors, two sets of stacked, sliding glass doors here and in the living-dining area open to the wraparound concrete deck.

In the kitchen, metal dominates in silver or dark grey..

The two kitchen islands are clad in stainless steel..

In the dining room, clear-acrylic zigzag chairs and a Sputnik-style chandelier provide a shot of Mid-century cool.

How would you describe the architectural development in Los Angeles?

Los Angeles is still a town of eternal optimism and a city that is trying to not define itself in the traditional terms that cities have been defined. For instance, someone says "San Francisco" and you immediately have a mental picture, or "Boston", a different Picture. But say "Los Angeles" and you do not (at least I don't) get an image or vision of what that place is- and I think that has allowed some of the most creative things to happen.

Mr. Beuth's home is flawless. The clean lines, open spaces and relationship to the outdoors, is architectural perfection at its finest for California living. Can you tell me about this project and the overall design criteria?

The project technically was a remodel but the entire building was virtually demolished with the exception of foundations and the overall envelope- to maintain older entitlements. We wanted to create a stunning home that captures the unrelenting views of the Los Angeles Basin and also make a great comfortable and livable home that allows a variety of activities including the entertainment of guests and friends.

A custom walnut dining table stands on the other side of the limestone block.

The main level of the home is transparent with three glass elevations providing sweeping views of downtown L.A., the Getty Center, and the Pacific Ocean.

The walnut-floored living and dining areas are on one side of the staircase and the kitchen is on the other side of this continuous open space.

The visual cues throughout the home are solid and masculine in tone.

The bedroom and bath, finished in limestone, glass tile, and walnut, effectively appear as one space. Tell me about the bathroom.

The master bedroom shower is a clear glass box in the middle of the master suite-you can actually take a shower and see the city view and watch your lover who may still be in bed.

The club room was designed to include a dance floor, bar, DJ booth and mirrored disco ball.

Jeff's residence as an entertainment haven with posh amenities that include a ballroom, screening room, billiards room, and glass-walled pool.

This showpiece makes a comfortable home that allows a variety of activities ideal for entertaining.

Glass is as clear as possible to meet the energy and solar needs.

Ludwig Mies van der Rohe's white leather Barcelona daybed and chairs provide seating.

In this design, color plays little role.

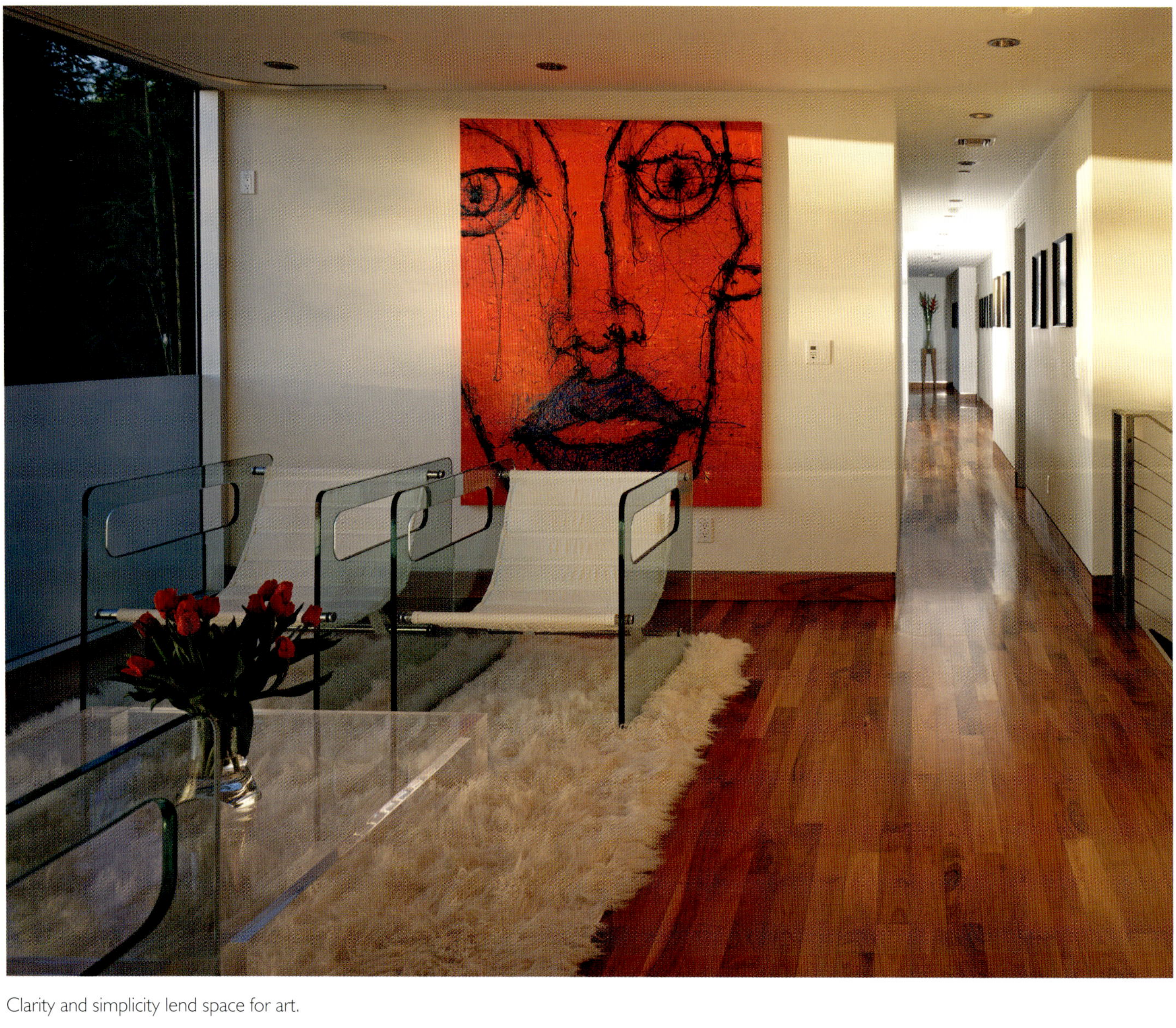

Clarity and simplicity lend space for art.

How would you describe the success of this project?

Unexpected. I thought that it was just a job that I was doing, simply to put food on the table and it turned out great. I have to give a tremendous amount of credit to the owner who was as obsessed about details as any architect would be – and in the end his outfitting of the project with the furnishings and interior design elements is on par with any interior designer that I have ever worked with.

The client wanted a window between the pool and the "pool room."

The master bedroom shower is a clear glass box in the middle of the master suite-you can actually take a shower and see the city view and watch your lover who may still be in bed.

The project technically was a remodel, but the entire building was virtually demolished with the exception of foundations and the overall envelope to maintain older entitlements.

The architects created a bold structure to capture unrelenting views of the Los Angeles basin.

BOOTYLICIOUS

Interview with Designer Don Stewart of Desiderata on the home of Hollywood bachelor Kanye West

Kanye's office has a custom colored leather Eames chair, a Maurice Culca plastic desk and colored pillows by Murakami.

Designer Don Stewart, owner of Desiderata in Los Angeles, renovated musician Kanye West's Hollywood Hills home. Kanye, who is a passionate about art and design, has a home, which is full of surprise and color. Don Stewart answers the following questions.

Tell me about the overall design scope for Kanye's home?

Well, it started out as furnishings, carpets and drapes. What it turned into was a complete renovation. When Kanye bought the home it was basically a big box -a three story contemporary with low cost materials on a vertical lot. It had the potential of fantastic views but had standard scale windows and doors. We simplified the design, tightened up the box and increased the view opportunities with Fleetwood windows throughout. What you now have is a very low profile, minimalist structure hidden behind an ivory panel of steel.

In this room there is an Arne sofa, an Igloo chair, a swivel coffee table from Twentieth, and a custom-made rug. The "Jetsons " was commissioned and painted by Burton Morris.

This job must have been enjoyable for you. Looking at Kanye's office – its such a colorful room to hang out in! It looks very animated like something you might see in a 3D cartoon. What can you tell me about the art piece?

That's a Marilyn silkscreen by Russell Young. When we were looking at furnishings Kanye had a strong response to the Marilyn painting, he had to have it. And I'm thinking, "Hmm, you really like Marilyn? ... hot pink? Well, there is a cross in the background on the hill...?" So I'm talking to him about it and I ask him, "What is it you like most about it?" "That's what I see!" is his response... Ahh! New perspective for me... he was identifying with the massive crowd, the audience.

The Kitchen was a complete renovation. The designer incorporated a custom floating lacquer cabinet on the wall, new raw plaster walls/ceilings and new French walnut floors.

Mixing it up with new and vintage, comfort is key in the living room.

"Working with musicians can be crazy-making, but it's also really fun since they are usually creative and open to do some really cool stuff," states designer Don Stewart.

The intimate bedroom offers fantastic views.

I've worked with musicians as well and understand that creating a space for someone who travels a lot can be tricky. Decisions need to be made in a timely manner to stay on track with the design work and we strive to work as efficiently as possible to ensure that our client has a great place to come home to. How were you able to execute this project and do you have any advice for other designers?

You're right! Working with musicians can be crazy-making, but it's also really fun since they are usually creative and open to do some really cool stuff. The absence of the artist from their space is not necessarily the greatest barrier for me in achieving our goal, so long as we remain in direct communication at all times in the interest of the project. No managers, no assistants, no publicists, no agents and no housekeepers. Directly with the client! That's my advice to anyone in this business.

What started out as a small job, turned into a complete renovation for the bathroom.

The master bedroom is low-profile minimalism.

This home has clean lines and is masculine yet relaxing and fun. Can you comment on your own overall impressions on the success of this project?

For me, the success of this project is reflected in seeing Kanye slipping around in his socks with laptop in hand and just being home, enjoying his space.

A crystal chandelier is juxtaposed with a steamer trunk and prints of Campbell's soup cans by Andy Warhol.

Kanye's private entry into the master suite.

Kanye, passionate about art and design, is seen in his dining room.

TAKE YA HOME

Interview with Interior Designer Courtney Carol Small on the home of Hollywood bachelor David Naylor

Raised in California and educated in Paris, Interior designer Courtney Carol Small began her career as a fashion editor for Allure Magazine. Eventually she started designing interiors for private clients and established a design firm catering to entertainment industry clientele.

Her client, David Naylor, owns DNA, a production company that has produced music videos for many divas like Madonna, Janet Jackson, J-Lo, Britney Spears and Shakira. I once read an article in the *New York Times* saying that *"no man holds a candle to David Naylor, Hollywood's bachelor nonpareil."* Courtney talks about David Naylor's West Hollywood home.

David actually cooks, but as a single man he didn't require a huge amount of storage.

The living room was inspired by the Chateau Marmont, within walking distance of David's house.

This is an example of early 20th century architecture and I understand David was meticulous about having it restored. What did you need to do for him?

David hired me to redo the living room but I ended up remodeling the kitchen and master bath - painting, detailing and refurnishing the entire house, top to bottom.

I find it interesting how I, as a woman designer, tend to become more maternal when I have a single male client. I find myself baking cookies or pies and bringing them to him – knowing he truly appreciates it. I also feel a greater sense of taking care of his home during the working process. Do you have similar experiences?

David's house was my first project done for a "stranger". It was done back in the day when I was a one-man-show and did project's one-on-one and one at a time. I would show up everyday, put his coffee cup in the dishwasher and tidy up, before going over everything that was being done by the carpenter or painter or worker of the day. When speaking to the various contractors I would (and still do) use the word we, and after about six months they were shocked to learn that I didn't live at the house or own the house, but was the interior designer. I just took ownership of the project and it was as personal to me as it was to David.

Looking at David's home, you can see that this is a space for someone who is definitely unpretentious and down to earth.

David has a black vintage stove that he loves. The original pale yellow wall tile remains in his kitchen.

The living room feels very cozy, was this inspired from somewhere?

David's house is within walking distance of one of his favorite haunts, the Chateau Marmont. The living room is set up to be as comfortable as a men's smoking club, or an extension of the Chateau's lounge.

Looking at David's place, the atmosphere is one of warmth, personality and comfort. You can also see that this is a home for someone who is definitely unpretentious and down to earth.

Dreamy landscape photographs collected by David was the inspiration for the home's paint palette of soft grey, browns and muddy yellow.

Courtney replaced the original pink sink and tub with the exact period originals in white.

WHERE THE PARTY AT?

Interview with Interior designer Kari Whitman on the home of Hollywood bachelor Dave Levine

Designed as a space for additional entertaining, a beautiful effect was created in the bathroom by installing Pulp Studio Glass - an Asian paper that is pressed between two sheets of glass.

Kari Whitman, interior designer, creates living spaces throughout the United States. Traveling frequently throughout the world, Kari stays abreast of eclectic products and trends, offering many styles of interiors that are both functional and beautiful. Her clientele, largely celebrity based, includes Jessica Alba, Virginia Madsen, Emilio Estevez and Don Henley. Her bachelor client, millionaire Dave Levine, lives in a view home in the Sunset Plaza area of West Hollywood. Interest in sex toys (bolstered by features in the *Sex and the City* television series) have garnered this bachelor's rapid financial growth for his internet based company Sextoy.com.

Dave loves to entertain and he wanted a comfortable, masculine home that would be "party proof."

Tell me about the home you created for Dave.

Dave loves to entertain and he wanted a comfortable, masculine space
that was "party proof"—something that would look fantastic and withstand his
busy social schedule. I created an elegant, masculine and entirely livable space
that easily accommodates lots of guests and has the durability to hold up party after party.

An elegant, masculine and entirely livable space was created that can easily accommodate lots of guests.

Was there anything unusual that he wanted for his home?

Yes! He wanted to have a very large living area designated for entertaining, and I designed it around a stripper pole that was installed. We also needed to remodel the kitchen to accommodate modern appliances and create a more efficient space for entertaining large parties.

Dave's bathroom is interesting, especially the bathtub/ What were his wishes?

He wanted a bathtub/steam shower for entertaining. I created a space that is both elegant and meets the" extracurricular" needs of my client, so I think the bathroom is outrageously successful!

The kitchen needed to be functional as well as have the ability to withstand Dave's busy social schedule.

The view of the city from Dave's terrace overlooks the city.

Is Dave happy with the finished house?

He wanted a place where he could entertain in style and comfort. I created an elegant, masculine and entirely livable space that easily accommodates lots of guests. My client reports that he's never had more success with women as he does now.

Reworked to make room for entertaining, the kitchen was remodeled to include modern appliances and room for entertaining.

The designer used a color scheme of brown, blue and recycled teak flooring.

A guest bathroom was created to be both masculine and elegant.

Interview with interior designer Kathryn Waltzer on the home of Hollywood bachelor Dr. Hayworth

Los Angeles interior designer Kathryn Waltzer is known for creating interiors that convey a sophisticated and stylish aesthetic with a fresh interpretation and signature touch. Kathryn cares about her client and feels that no matter what is happening in the outside world her client's home is a grounding point for his life. Kathryn's client, Dr. Hayworth, is a celebrity cosmetic surgeon for Fox TV's make-over show "The Swan". His 1925 Mediterranean home is situated in West Hollywood – in an area with great views of Hollywood and beyond. Kathryn talks with me about this project.

Dr. Hayworth's home is a great example of one of the many diverse styles of architecture that was designed in the last century. Did he have specific requests that needed to be incorporated into the project?

The entire project needed to be utilized for entertaining, both for intimate and large-scale events.

The art work in the living room is fascinating. Can you tell me about any of these pieces?

It is the client's art collection. He is passionate about art and is an artist himself. He's a member of MOCA's Board of Acquisitions. The impressionistic piece was painted by his mother. The medium in the piece over the chaise is blood.

The home interior was designed for entertaining, both for intimate and large-scale events. Photo by D. Vorillon.

The entry walls have squares of faux-parchment paper with an overglaze Photo by D. Vorillon

As a doctor, the owner is a healer and the colors used reflect warmth, gentleness, and subtlety. Photo by D. Vorillon.

The idea behind this design was to assemble sophisticated spaces for a man of Dr. Hayworth's taste, and create a home where he would feel utterly comfortable. Photo by D. Vorillon.

Dr. Hayworth is passionate about art and is an artist himself. Photo by D. Vorillon

In talking about color, you mentioned that the color palette you selected reflected the client's personality, in what way?

As a doctor he is a healer, and the color reflects warmth, gentleness and subtlety. On his classic and sophisticated side, the color echoes a cultured, masculine understanding of fashion, the arts and all things fine.

A lot of designers have commented that when they have a client who is a single man, he may depend on them more for guidance and design decisions; have you had that experience as well, and did you have it with this project?

He was far less needy than my typical bachelor client although, in typical bachelor fashion, he needed me more than he thinks he did.

A terra cotta tone was added to the walls to create a more intimate yet festive space for dining. Photo by D. Vorillon

ME & U

Interview with architect Patrick Tighe on the home of Hollywood bachelor Michael Collins

Tighe Architecture principal, Patrick Tighe, is an award winning architect committed to contemporary as well as innovative design. He extensively remodeled an existing residence in West Hollywood, for art dealer, Michael Collins. This house is situated in a residential street a few houses in from Robertson Boulevard, a popular area for shops and galleries. Patrick took an uninspired house and transformed it into a functional yet comfortable retreat.

The home was designed to offer a great sense of seclusion and tranquility.

The interiors as well as the exterior courtyard and reflecting pool all together create a wonderful urban oasis.

This house is situated in a residential street a few houses in from Robertson Boulevard, a popular area for shops and galleries.

Patrick, how would you describe this home?

The project questions residential architecture by blending the public function of an art gallery with the domestic components of a house. The new building accommodates the needs of the residents as well as large gatherings.

A new load-bearing wall was introduced that bisects the building on the diagonal.

The clerestory serves as the main light source, eliminating the need for windows.

Patrick took an uninspired house and transformed it into a functional yet comfortable retreat.

The fireplace front, used for showing art, is a continuation of the tilted roof plane.

The project questions residential architecture by blending the public function of an art gallery with the domestic components of a house.

Paintings are displayed on the ledge of the fireplace mantel.

The challenge was to create a spacious gallery space within a relatively small building envelope.

In the dining area, seating is arranged to enjoy the art.

Quiet and private, the master bedroom opens to the garden.

The master bathroom is understated and tranquil.

This area of West Hollywood can be tight, did you have restraints?

The challenge was to create a spacious gallery space within a relatively small building envelope. The existing site condition consisted of a 1400 sq. ft residence on a 4000 sq. ft lot. The existing structure was of sub standard construction and had no architectural significance. City regulations required that the square footage and footprint of the existing structure be maintained. A minimum of fifty-percent of the existing walls was to remain intact. The solution was a scale appropriate response that was in keeping with the neighboring buildings.

The mirror detail in the master bath reflects the shower.

Michael's 'children' in the bathtub.

I had a shop nearby on Robertson so I'm very familiar with that neighborhood. It's a mix of early 20th century architecture, so I understand the challenges in creating something new and contemporary. You're attempting to provide for your client's wishes as well as respecting the surrounding residences. How did you specifically plan the structure to house the art?

A new load-bearing wall was introduced that bisects the building on the diagonal. Two distinct zones were created differentiating the gallery from the residence and separating the public from the private functions. The roof plane of the gallery was lifted allowing light to enter the gallery. The clerestory serves as the main light source, eliminating the need for windows and maximizing wall surface for the display of art.

How would you describe the living areas?

The domestic zone consists of 2 bedrooms, 2 bathrooms and a kitchen. All components are accessed from the main gallery space. Sliding partitions of opaque laminated glass close off the rooms from the gallery.

This is a very alluring home. The interiors as well as the exterior courtyard and reflecting pool all together create a wonderful urban oasis, offering a great sense of seclusion and tranquility.

Two distinct zones were created differentiating the gallery from the residence.

The master bedroom has views of the private back yard.

The domestic zone consists of two bedrooms, two bathrooms, and a kitchen. All components are accessed from the main gallery space.

Michael and a friend sit on the back porch with 'his kids.'

SHOW STOPPER

Interview with XTEN Architects on the home of Hollywood bachelor Randolph Duke

XTEN Architecture is a well known architecture firm in Los Angeles, as well as in Basel, Switzerland where their satellite office is located. Its founding partners, Monika Häfelfinger and Austin Kelly, work in a distinctive method to development contemporary architecture. The emphasis is on minimalist logic, material transformation and refined detailing and craftsmanship. Their work has appeared extensively in print and *Architectural Record Magazine* recognized them as one of twelve Emerging Architects to watch. The following home was designed by Xten for Hollywood fashion designer Randolph Duke, whose gowns have been on academy award winners such as Angelina Jolie and Hilary Swank.

Randolph Duke has the fortune of enjoying nature from all levels of his home.

This property, originally a three-lot promontory site looks precarious and difficult to design a structure for it.

This was a challenging site to integrate. But, we were successful in that we created a structure which integrated into the landscape as well as being open to the city below.

Awesome city vistas are seen from the master bedroom.

The glass is anchored by solid sculptural elements like the concrete main stair.

This property, originally a three-lot promontory site looks precarious and difficult to design a structure for it.

The views are fantastic and the design has taken full advantage of these sweeping vistas.

A view of the front fountain.

The views are amazing and your design work has taken full advantage of these sweeping views. Describe the configuration of the structure itself.

The large first-floor platform cantilevers out over the hillside and also embeds itself into the hill. The second story just sort of floats over that." The stepped and suspended volume, containing open living spaces on the first floor and a master suite on the second, project from the hill to hover above the city like a pair of wings.

The skin of the house, such as it is, consists largely of 10-foot-high glass panels that slide open to erase all boundaries between indoors and out.

The landscape can be viewed from the kitchen as well.

The front, side, and rear elevations of the house slide open to erase all boundaries between indoors and out. From the sitting area, the space connects to the gardens.

Xten designed this residence of Hollywood fashion designer Randolph Duke, whose gowns have been on academy award winners such as Angelina Jolie and Hilary Swank.

As seen from the dining room, this structure was integrated into the landscape as well as being open to the city below.

Randolph has the fortune of enjoying nature from all levels.

Retaining walls, not only utilized to extend the first floor living level into the hillside but also provide the hardscape for gardens on two levels. As well, the front, side, and rear elevations of the house slide open to erase all boundaries between indoors and out, connecting the spaces to the gardens on both levels.

The interior colors of primarily black and white with secondary color of browns, pale blues, and creams play well against the landscapes. What materials were used?

For the floors, a material made of light quartz stones set in an epoxy base was used. A charcoal plaster along with dark rift-cut oak was installed on the walls and flat-cut black-diamond granite was used to clad the fireplace.

A view of the home as it sits precariously on the property.

A charcoal plaster along with dark rift-cut oak was installed on the walls and flat-cut black-diamond granite was used to clad the fireplace.

The skin of the house, such as it is, consists largely of 10- foot-high glass panels that slide open to erase all boundaries between indoors and out. The glass is anchored by solid sculptural elements like a concrete main stair, planes of dark stucco and wood paneling and a monumental stacked-stone fireplace that connects the two floors and penetrates the glass to link the interior and exterior. All in all, it is a stellar example of 21st century architecture.

A view of the glass tiles surrounding the master bath.

The floors, as seen in the tub area, are a material made of light quartz stones set in an epoxy base.

The side garden offers an extended area for entertaining.

Chapter 4

PAST THE VELVET ROPES

***"During your life, never stop dreaming. No one can take away your dreams."* — Tupac Shakur**

The name Hollywood, legend has it, was coined by a young couple in the late 1800s who recorded the term on one of the first real estate subdivisions in Los Angeles. In the early 20th century much of this land was still barren, inhabited by citrus groves and one hotel, which has since been replaced by the Kodak Theater – home to the Academy Awards. Through the past century diverse styles of homes have popped up as well as the building of five major film studios. Today, while Paramount Pictures is the only major remaining studio in this area (the others have dispersed to other sections of Los Angeles) Hollywood is enjoying a revival with trendy bars, nightclubs, luxury homes, loft and condominium redevelopments, and restored hotels.

Tinsel town at night

Directly east of Hollywood are the Los Feliz and Silver Lake communities. Los Feliz is home to the iconic Griffith Observatory. Neighboring Silver Lake is known for it's bohemian vibe, where writers, artists and musicians such as Jane's Addiction, Red Hot Chili Peppers and Tom Waits have lived. The hillsides surrounding Silver Lake's manmade reservoir are filled with original structures built in the 1930s, 40s and 50s by avant-garde modernist like architects R.M. Schindler, Raphael Soriano, John Lautner, and Richard Neutra.

Drive south east and you'll enter downtown Los Angeles, which has been depicted in films like *Transformers, Collateral, Independence Day* and *The Terminator*. This area has become a hip destination for its arts and cultural centers (The Museum of Contemporary Art, Walt Disney Concert Hall, Nokia Theater, and the Staple Sports Center for the Lakers and Clippers Professional basketball teams) along with enclaves of revitalized lofts and luxury apartment complexes. Drinking in the nightlife fun, in hotels such as the Standard, one might bump into guys like Justin Timberlake, Kiefer Sutherland or Mario Lopez. Creative energy drives the bachelors whose homes you will view in this chapter.

A view inside the club scene

Hollywood Star Walk

The energy of Downtown

ROLL WITH IT

Interview with designer Michael Morten Neumayr on the home of Hollywood bachelor Tom Whitman

This home was created as a space for Tom to relax in and get a way from all the bustle of his busy life.

Austrian native, Michael Morten Neumayr, balances fusion of his Danish- Austrian cultural background, American education, and his affinity for Asian philosophy and spirituality. Certified in Qi-Mag Feng Shui, Michael incorporates this knowledge in all of his designs to create environments that emulate well-being and bring on a sense of simplistic beauty and peace. His Silver Lake client, Tom Whitman, is a Hollywood promoter and producer whose concerts have showcased entertainers such as Britney Spears, Whitney Houston and The Backstreet Boys. The following is a discussion with Michael reflecting on his work.

Tom's goal for the kitchen was to have massive counter space and a bar like area to be able to serve food and drinks for parties.

I think it's intriguing that you utilize Qi-Mag Feng Shui into your practice. Fifteen years ago, when I began Qigong studies in relation to Chinese medicine, the Asian monasteries were just beginning to allow the Taoist masters to teach theses disciplines to Western civilization. Through the years we now are seeing many variations of eastern traditions and practices blend into Western culture like Feng Shui, for example. Michael, can you briefly explain the idea of what Qi-Mag Feng Shui is?

Qi-Mag Feng Shui is a fusion of different ancient eastern and western traditions. Its main purpose is to create an environment that emanates serenity and harmony. My clients say they have found more joy, improved health, and have become more productive and successful as well as having more harmonious relationships.

Ok, that sounds really interesting and I assume we would need a longer conversation to fully understand how that works. When you started on this home for your client what specific design solutions needed to be incorporated into this project?

The room, where the kitchen was initially located, was to be made twice as large, since the kitchen should become the center of the house, offering plenty of space for entertaining guests. The client, who is an artist and photographer, wished to have a clean and easy flow through the house and plenty of art walls to hang his extensive art collection. Furthermore, he put a lot of emphasis to transforming the much-neglected backyard into a casual serene entertainment area with an expansive wood deck and a recently added pool and Jacuzzi area to create an Asian feel. The outdoor lounge was to be positioned in such a way that you could have a great view of LA's best-known landmark, the Hollywood sign.

The color scheme was to be natural such as dark floors and dark materials for the furnishings.

The client's wish was to have a clean and easy flow through the house.

I've always said that size doesn't matter. You've proven that by making the most of a small bathroom. What were your thoughts to achieve this?

The master bathroom is relatively small in size. Mr. Whitman wanted to have something unique and a very graphic design concept and an almost stringent attention to detail, with no superfluous details or gadgets standing around, to give him a clear visual surrounding when he starts his day.

What elements provided the sanctuary environment for Tom?

My client has a very busy and interesting life, so he was looking to create a space, to relax and get away from life's bustle. My first solution to address this wish was the design of the front patio. Big black slate stepping stones set in a bed of white marble gravel, leading the way to the front door, automatically slow down you pace when you come home. The trickling sound of water emanates from a fountain, also offering tranquility the moment you enter the house. The second solution was to create a meditative lounge area with a fire pit in the backyard, where he could sit, relax and meditate, while looking across his lush garden to see the Hollywood Sign on the Horizon.

It appears that you were successful in achieving a Shangri-La for your client.

The master bedroom was expanded to include more space, a lot of light and a great view into his magnificent garden.

In the bathroom, the client wanted a simple room that would give him a clear visual surrounding when he starts his day.

Tom wanted to transform a much neglected backyard into a casual serene entertainment area.

SATISFACTION

Interview with designer Chet Callahan regarding the home of Hollywood bachelor Jacinto Hernandez

Walls, closets, and hallways were removed to open the spaces to each other and to the views of the Los Angeles River basin, the Santa Monica Mountains, the Griffith Observatory, and the Hollywood sign outside.

Chet Callahan is a designer who believes that each project site has a unique character and his goal is to respect that character, while adapting the site to respond to his client's needs.

His client, financier Jacinto Hernandez, lives in the hills with views of Griffith Observatory. Chet, of Chet Callahan Design talks about this home he designed for client, "Jase".

The Hills here are one of the best places to live in Los Angeles and Jase has a great house with amazing views.

He does now. In the renovation, walls, closets, and hallways were removed to open the spaces to each other for the views.

What was the overall design scope for this project?

View House is a 1,600 square foot two story box, cantilevered 40'-0" beyond the Hollywood Hills. The original floor plan divided the clear span structure into three bedrooms, two and a half bathrooms, a galley kitchen, and a fireplace which served as a barricade to the sweeping views outside. The end product is a complete renovation of the existing 1,600 square foot house that better conforms to the client's lifestyle and creates a pleasing frame from which to view Los Angeles beyond.

A once cramped Master Bathroom became a water closet and shower room, now flanked by a generous dressing and wash area. The free-standing soaking tub, vertical grain white oak millwork, French limestone floors, and expansive view offer a welcome respite from the city below.

Architects are agreeing that it can be easier working for a single man than say a couple.

It is great having a single point of contact and a single point of view to relate to-- not only in the design, but in the presentation of the design.

The kitchen complements Jase very well and allows him to display his personality from the cooking island in the center of the main living space.

Natural, muted finishes bring contrast to the landscape beyond the house and the colorful objects—including the client within it.

View House is the natural residence for a very unique client with spectacular surroundings.

In the renovation, two bedrooms merged to become the Master Suite.

For this project, was there anything interesting about it that appealed to you best?

The place itself is awe-inspiring as the sweeping views of the Los Angeles River basin, the Santa Monica Mountains, the Griffith Observatory, and the Hollywood sign outside are breath-taking. In hindsight, I was given great freedom in my creativity, but it never felt that way. View House is the natural residence for a very unique client with spectacular surroundings.

TURN OFF THE LIGHT

Interview with Designer, Heidi Toll on the home of Hollywood bachelor Dave Navarro

Heidi Toll, a designer whom *Interior Design Magazine* dubbed one of the top ten "designers to watch," has a sense of style that appeals to clients who seek class and sophistication. A believer in sustainable design, her firm was one of the first in the country to focus on the use of "green" materials.

Her Client is musician Dave Navarro, famous for his performance work with Red Hot Chili Peppers and Jane's Addiction. Heidi created Dave's home, a loft space in an iconic part of Hollywood- at the corner of Hollywood and Vine with views of the Hollywood sign and Capitol Records

Dave has been quoted as saying he "wanted clothes to literally fall off a girl". With this sense of humor, color was introduced to punctuate a certain mood.

Heidi, What do you think are the most important determinants that have guided interior design development in Los Angeles?

There can be no question that Los Angeles is a primary driver of "green" design. Our connection to the ocean and outdoor living is a constant reminder that what we use and subsequently dispose of impacts the world around us. And of course we are the cradle of mid-century modern architecture as the birthplace of most of the Case Study homes and the canvas upon which great architects such as Neutra, Koenig and A. Quincy Jones created some of their most famous works. Those sensibilities not only persist today, but are regaining popularity.

For Dave Navarro's home, how would you summarize the overall design criteria?

Dave has a strong modernist streak and he came to us wanting something clean and minimal, but also something that complemented his "rock and roll" bachelor lifestyle. The trick was, we had only two weeks to move him in! So we addressed the project in two phases. First, we located furnishings that were more or less in stock and that looked sleek and tasteful but with a little sass. Then we moved him in after two weeks. Then we had some fun infusing a touch of the client's sexy, rock n' roll personality into the space through accessories.

We were inspired to introduce a bit of the "animal" side of Dave through certain elements. This is a cold-rolled steel dining table base with a faux python top under glass.

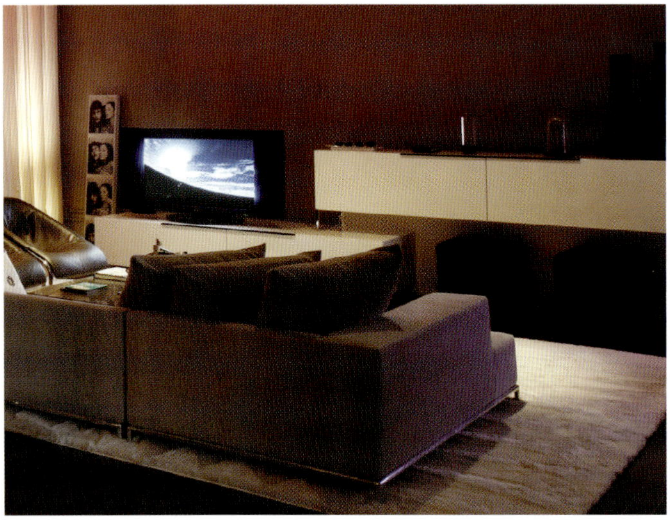

One of the nice things about our design and the manner in which we programmed the space is that it can completely change mood and character depending on the lighting.

Dave's guitar takes a break.

We had some fun infusing a touch of the client's sexy, rock n' roll personality into the space through accessories.

I have found that working with a musician can be fun yet challenging as they travel a lot, so it can be difficult to get together with him on design decisions. How did this process work out for Dave and yourself?

I have to say, it was actually easier for us when we did Dave's first house while he was on tour. We got to do all the messy work when he wasn't around and present an entire finished product upon his return. In this case, Dave was out for shorter appearances only. There's inevitably stages in the process that may not look so great, or where all the pieces haven't yet arrived that pull an area together and stuff can look out-of-place and Dave got to see all of that which he claims he enjoyed – like Christmas every day. But I know there must have been times when he was wondering how things were going to turn out and I'd rather present only the finished product to clients whenever possible.

Did Dave have any unusual requests?

When you're not just a bachelor but also a rock star, the bedroom can be a very, um, significant feature. Since Dave's loft is one large, open space, we wanted to come up with a way to set the bed area apart and make it special without breaking the space up by building walls. There was a recessed area of the loft that seemed like the natural place to create a bedroom, and we worked with that. A custom white vinyl platform bed, a black crystal chandelier with dark red light bulbs, and sparkly sheer drapery complete the space for privacy.

Color is a very interesting topic, especially in terms of what a client wants.

Color holds a more precious position with Dave than it does with most clients. He travels a lot and loves the peaceful feeling he gets from rooms at luxury hotels. Consequently, he likes his house to feel mostly very neutral- a very clean palate. Where there is great contrast it is often achieved with black and white – which I find can be even more dramatic than color if introduced properly. So color was introduced to punctuate a certain mood we were trying to support – which I might characterize as sexy and sultry, but Dave has been quoted as saying he "wanted clothes to literally fall off a girl" when she came into the room, which, by the way, is a great little peek into how great a sense of humor he has and how much fun he is as a client. To that end, we stayed in a mostly red/purple theme- a persimmon chair, plum mohair ottomans, red vases and a red bathroom ceiling.

Do you feel your project was successful?

Yes. We finished it on time and on budget and created a happy client who loves to be in this very personal space.

The famed Capitol Records building can be seen from the dining area.

The final touch in the bed area is a black crystal chandelier with dark red light bulbs.

We created a miniature gallery space out of the entry and chose a twinkling black glass bead Maya Romanoff wall covering for this purpose.

Dave has a strong modernist streak and he came to us wanting something clean and minimal, but also something that complemented his "rock and roll" bachelor lifestyle.

FLOAT ON

Interview with architects Harvey Fleming Watts & James Schwentker on the home of Hollywood bachelor Steve Johnson

Harvey Fleming Watts and James Schwentker, principals of Schwentker Watts Design, are based in Silverlake and create residential architecture and landscape design in a range of styles that foremost strive to work closely with each client. Their projects have included the homes of director Michael Bay, television writer/producer David Lee, and actress Ellen DeGeneres.

Harvey & James talk about their client, special effects professional Steve Johnson, whose contribution to film is a diverse repertoire including *War of the Worlds* and *Cat in the Hat*.

Steve collaborated in pushing towards a more experimental approach of design while respecting the original character of the handsome Spanish revival house.

This was an extensive remodel which included the gardens, terraces and rear courtyard as well as the swimming pool, spa and fountain.

The wonderful U-shaped hillside Spanish style house sits on a property that is terraced and ascend up from the street.

The enormous, and equally over-scaled mature avocado tree balances the space – the second floor terrace and stair allows one to "climb" the tree and experience the space in three dimensions.

Interview with Architect, Jennifer Siegal of OMD

Jennifer Siegal is founder and principal of the Los Angeles' based firm Office of Mobile Design (OMD), which is dedicated to the design and construction of modern, sustainable and precision-built structures. With a master's degree from the Southern California Institute of Architecture (SCI-Arc), she is the inaugural Julius Shulman Institute Fellow at Woodbury University. Her innovative design sensibilities and expertise in futuristic concepts, prefabricated construction, and green building technologies were recognized by the popular media in 2003 when *Esquire* named her one of the design world's "Best and Brightest". Jennifer talks about the project she designed for a bachelor living in downtown Los Angeles.

Tell me about this structure.

This 3,000 square foot residence is situated in a 300 loft live-work artist community by the Brewery. Industrial and traditional materials are playfully combined, using storage containers and steel found on-site in downtown LA.

This home, appears organic and is filled with light.

Large panels of glass throughout the house open up the space, allowing natural light to pour in, connecting it to the private garden oasis and artists' community. This home literally grows up from the land around it, engaging with and incorporating the industrial history of downtown LA by using found-on-site materials.

Grain trailers helped transformed this property into a beautiful home.

The home connects to the private garden oasis as well as to the artists' community

This 3,000 square foot residence is situated in a 300 loft live-work artist community by the Brewery.

Here, recycled materials are not just practical and cost-effective; they create a unique, dramatic architectural vocabulary.

The design you implemented works well for this structure. You are known for your approach of utilizing new materials and forms to create architecture. What materials were used here?

Grain trailers were transformed into koi fishponds and a lap pool. The storage containers were used to create and separate the dwelling spaces within the house. Each storage container has its own individual function, one is the entertainment and library area, another is a dining room and office space overlooking the garden below, another serves as the bathroom and laundry room, and yet another is the master bedroom, a visually dramatic protruding volume that wraps around the upper part of the house.

Utilizing recycled materials are not only practical and cost-effective but create a unique, dramatic architectural vocabulary. Combined with steel and glass, the result is sculptural, open and LA modern. What a surprising addition to the landscapes of downtown.

Industrial and traditional materials are playfully combined, using storage containers and steel found on-site in downtown LA.

The kitchen is both functional and aesthetically balanced.

Engaged with and incorporating the industrial history of downtown LA by using found-on-site materials, this home literally grows up from the land around it.

Large storage containers are used to create and separate the dwelling spaces within the house.

TEMPTED TO TOUCH

Interview with Architect, Aleks Istanbullu regarding the home of Hollywood bachelor Paul Solomon

Aleks Istanbullu Architects is an award-winning professional design studio with aesthetic foundations rooted in the Modernism of Europe, Chicago, and Southern California. They are a creative team of architects committed to producing contemporary architecture. Their process distills each design premise to a core set of requirements and desires. Within this context, they craft buildings that last and inspire. They respect the nature of materials, both traditional and new, carefully detailing their buildings to celebrate the craft of their profession while optimizing the effectiveness of current technologies and labor. The following is a conversation about Aleks's work and his client, Paul Solomon, a visionary developer who resides in Arts District of downtown LA.

Paul Solomon, a visionary developer, resides in this home located in the Arts District of downtown Los Angeles.

Aleks, what is the philosophy that drives you?

Architecture is a process through which we make space. Simplicity and directness fascinate me. I believe design that is infused with content will have lasting meaning. With regard to working with existing buildings, I believe that if we respect the past, the future will respect us.

What inspired you to practice architecture?

The desire to control my environment.

What do you think are the most important determinants that have guided architectural development in Los Angeles?

Variety. Although this has historically been seen due to a lack of cohesiveness, it is now being seen as an asset. As opposed to a wonderful city like Chicago, which is architecturally cohesive, Los Angeles' discordant nature is now more reflective of the diversity of our culture.

Is there a particular space in Los Angeles that you'd take someone to if you were going to show them the perfect LA space or moment?

L.A.'s St. Elmo Village, an African America artist community for which I have volunteered services over the last 15 years and on whose board I serve. The old Mary Pickford stables that have been converted to work units for artists and a series of classrooms where the artists teach in exchange for cheap rent, providing pro bono after school art education to neighborhood children.

Paul's wishes were "cool" design and something that felt good to him.

The amazing master bathroom is a combination of masculinity as well as sensuality.

This was truly a loft design in the sense that the architect's responsibility was the sinuous hard construction in the center of the space.

Paul had a special request of installing a claw foot tub.

In defining this loft, the architects introduced a freestanding sensuous object that eludes geometric definition.

How would you describe the space your created for Paul, as well as the ethereal sense you put into it?

This is a loft space, and we introduced a freestanding sensuous object that eludes geometric definition and hopefully has a chance of being ethereal.

Was there an unusual request that Paul had?

The client wanted to use a claw foot tub.

I really admire your work and consider this to be a notable space to live in. How would you describe the success of your project?

It feels open and intriguing. To me, it feels like some of the surreal photographs of the early 10th century raw spaces by Corb and Molino.

This existing warehouse space has a beautiful concrete structure and finish. The only colors we introduced were the white walls and the natural woods.

RESOURCES

CHAPTER 1 ***VISONS OF SAND AND WATER***

THE REMEDY Kanner Architects
1558 10th Street
Santa Monica 90401
info@kannerarch.com
Photography by John Linden

THE SPACE BETWEEN Kanner Architects
info@kannerarch.com
Photography by John Linden

OBSESSION Johnna McHugh Interior Design
606 North Larchmont Blvd. # 201
Los Angeles Ca 90004
Tel 323.469.4515
Photography by Jim McHugh

SIMPLE THINGS Melinda Gray AIA
GRAYmatter architecture
639 East Channel Road
Santa Monica, CA 90402
Tel 310.454.7960 ww.graymatterarchitecture.com
Photography by Grey Crawford

OH WHAT A NIGHT Ehrlich Architects
10865 Washington Blvd
Culver City, CA 90232
(310) 838-9700 www.s-**ehrlich**.com
Photography by Benny Chan

DO IT TO IT Steve Glenn Living Homes
2910 Lincoln blvd
Santa Monica, CA 90405
Tel 310. 581. 8500
Photography by CJ Bergy Photographics/Sunshine Divis Photography

GIMME THAT Sant Architects Inc
1613 Abbot Kinney Blvd, Venice
Tel 310.396.1828 www.**santarchitects**.com
Photography by Art Gray

CHAPTER 2 ***PALM TREES, HEDGEROWS & BLING***

AMAZED Duncan Nicholas Architect
Nicholson Wirts Architects
3200 Airport Avenue #12
Santa Monica CA 90405
Tel 310.313.0928
Photography by Lisa Romerein

IRREPLACEABLE Archtecture Callas Shortridge
3621 Hayden Ave
Culver City, CA 90232
(310) 280-0404 www.**callas-shortridge**.com
Photography by Grey Crawford

PUT IT ON ME Dean Larkin Design
8225.5 Santa Monica Blvd
West Hollywood, CA 90046
(323) 654-7500 www.**deanlarkin**design.com
Photography by John Ellis

I LIKE IT Interiors by MRY Architects
www.moorerubleyudell.com
Photography by Art Gray

CH-CHECK IT OUT Archicture by Griffith Enright
*www.griffin**enrightarchitects**.com*
Photography by Griffith Enright

AS GOOD AS I ONCE WAS Aaron Torrence
aaron_torrence@designplusconstruction.com
Photography by Aaron Torrance

SHOW ME WHAT YOU GOT Marmol Radziner
marmol-*radziner.com*
Photography by Benny Chan

CHAPTER 3 ***PANORAMA OF THE CITY***

HIGHER SPF: architects
8609 Washington Blvd.
Culver City, CA 90232
Tel 310.558.0902
Photography by john linden; Juergen Nogai and Julius Shulman

BOOTYLICIOUS Designed by Desiderata
1600 Carmona Ave
Los Angeles, CA 90019
(323) 935-8889
Photography by Art Gray

TAKE YA HOME Interior design Courtney Small
courtneysmall@sbcglobal.net
Photography by Marc Royce

WHERE THE PARTY AT designer Kari Whitman
www.Kariwhitmaninteriors.com
Photography by Chris Lovey

EASY Kathryn Waltzer, ASID, CID
310.890.0712 www.kathrynwaltzer.com
Photography by Dominique Vorillon

ME & U Tighe Architects
1632 Ocean Park Blvd
Santa Monica, CA 90405
www.tighearchitecture.com
Photography by Art Gray

SHOW STOPPER XTen Architecture
201 S. Santa Fe Avenue Suite 202
Los Angeles, CA 90012
Tel 213 625 7002
Photography by Art Gray

CHAPTER 4 ***PAST THE VELVET ROPES***

ROLL WITH IT Neumayr Design LLC
2314 Teviot Street
Los Angeles CA 90039
Tel 323.662.9819 www.neumayrdesign.com
Photography by Michael Weschler

SATISFACTION Chet Callahan Architect
6946 Pacific View Drive
Los Angeles, CA 90068
323.810.2438 chet@chetcallahan.com
Photography by Art Gray

TURN OFF THE LIGHT Designed by Heidi Toll
info@heiditolldesign.com
Photography by Edward Duarte

FLOAT ON Schwentker Watts Architect
www.sch-wat.com
Photography by Schwentker Watts

DEJA VU OMD Corp
1725 Abbot Kinney Blvd
Venice, CA 90291
Tel 310.439.1129 www.designmobile.com
Photography by Undine Prohl; Daniel Hennessy

TEMPTED TO TOUCH Aleks Istanbullu
1659 11th Street, Suite 200
Santa Monica, CA 90404
Tel: 310 450.8246
Photography by J. Samuelson

Index
of Architects and Designers